HOT
SAUCE
NATION

· · · · · · · · · · · · · · · · · · · ·

AMERICA'S
BURNING
OBSESSION

· · · · · · · · · · · · · · · · · · · ·

DENVER NICKS

CHICAGO
REVIEW
PRESS

Copyright © 2017 by Denver Nicks
All rights reserved
First edition
Published by Chicago Review Press Incorporated
814 North Franklin Street
Chicago, Illinois 60610

ISBN 978-1-61373-184-0

Library of Congress Cataloging-in-Publication Data

Names: Nicks, Denver, author.
Title: Hot sauce nation : America's burning obsession / Denver Nicks.
Description: First edition. | Chicago, Illinois : Chicago Review Press,
    Incorporated, [2017] | Includes bibliographical references and index.
Identifiers: LCCN 2016004330 (print) | LCCN 2016013894 (ebook) | ISBN
    9781613731840 (trade paper) | ISBN 9781613731864 (adobe pdf) | ISBN
    9781613731871 (epub) | ISBN 9781613731857 (kindle)
Subjects: LCSH: Hot pepper sauces—United States. | Cooking, American. |
    Cooking (Hot pepper sauces)
Classification: LCC TX819.H66 N53 2017 (print) | LCC TX819.H66
(ebook) | DDC
    641.3/384—dc23
LC record available at http://lccn.loc.gov/2016004330

Cover design: Jonathan Hahn
Cover illustration: Vid Taylor
Interior layout: Nord Compo

Printed in the United States of America
5 4 3 2 1

CONTENTS

For Rebecca

ACKNOWLEDGMENTS

As always and above all I am grateful to the people too numerous to name here whose generosity with their time, their stories, and their hot sauce made this work possible. Not all of them made it into these pages, but all contributed to this project and I cannot thank them enough.

Yuval Taylor is a wise guide and the best kind of editor, one who makes the work not just better but a better version of itself. My friend, confidant, and frequent coconspirator Jim Fitzgerald, who is also my agent, was instrumental as always and in myriad ways at all points of this project. I am hopeless without the help of many individuals, but I am especially indebted to my culture guru Greg Hermann, my journalism consigliere Jay Newton-Small, my chief literary consultant Kaira Casey, and my senior snacks adviser the itinerant Aric S. Queen. I am also indebted to the many friends and strangers who directed me to various hot sauce–related stories and happenings, and to my transcriptionist Gail Morrison.

I depend on friends and family to keep a roof over my head while on the road and to stay reasonably sane. Tremendous thanks to Dianna Knost, Drew Baker, Garett Neudeck, Richard Weening, Victoria Leslie, David Nicks, Travis and Constance Nicks, Savannah Nicks, Spencer Livingston-Gainey, Joshua Murl Jones, Clay Dillow, Julie Niemi, Arlet Siordia, Josh and Bailey Czupryk, Matthew

Bengloff, Suzette Matthews, Eustace Harold Winn IV, Mitchell and Allison London, Keith Kobylka, Synthia Link, Tyler Fields, Natty Adams, Andrea Leitch, Don and Antonia, Amy Clovis, Todd Rose, Garett Haake, Sara Murray, and Shiner.

INTRODUCTION

Philosophers have often looked for the defining feature of humans—language, rationality, culture, and so on. I'd stick with this: Man is the only animal that likes Tabasco sauce.
                    —Dr. Paul Bloom, *HOW PLEASURE WORKS*

My dad lost his sense of taste while I was growing up. It happened gradually, as his allergies and malformed nasal cavity conspired over the years to strangle his sense of smell. That knocked the legs right out from under his ability to perceive flavor. Determined to get something out of his meals, he'd drench them in the only thing he could almost taste: Tabasco hot sauce. He'd use more of it every year, and after a while the stuff was everywhere in our home, an omnipresent condiment at family meals, which seemed to get spicier by the year too. My mom is a brilliant and industrious woman, but I wouldn't trust her with a can of SpaghettiOs; dad was the cook in our family.

Not many consumer products resonate through my childhood memories as strongly as Tabasco, that smoky, tangy red fireball packed into a tiny clear bottle. It reminds me of dad (who eventually had nasal surgery and regained his sense of taste but has never lost his love for heat) and his wild marathon cooking sessions, chopping up a spicy storm in our hectic kitchen; the ceremony of adding the final, personal touch to a nearly complete dish and the rite of passage in growing old enough to actually enjoy it; the time my best friend introduced me to the holy trinity of macaroni, cheese, and hot sauce; or the time I told my little brother that Tabasco was a kind of candy. He guzzled all the shots of it he could before it dawned on him that this was not candy, his mouth was on fire, and his brother was an asshole.

It's no accident that hot sauce looms so large in the nostalgic corner of my brain. From among all of our senses both smell and taste are capable of producing some of our clearest and most poignant memories. But, as you know if you've ever poured too heartily from the wrong bottle of hot sauce, taste and smell are but secondary pieces of the hot sauce puzzle. There's something else happening with hot sauce unique to the chilies that are its essential ingredient, something weirder and kinkier and a stubborn mystery that cuts to the heart of what it means to be human—pain.

It's said he was a brave man who first ate an oyster. But what about the second man to eat a chili? Braver yet, I'd say. Eating an oyster is a bold proposition indeed, and far be it from me to disparage the mettle of that industrious and no doubt very hungry person, but the queer-looking clam is, in the end, a pretty innocuous mark. It tastes either good or bad before it slithers down the gullet, and that's about the end of it.

Now picture the scene before our curious prehistoric foodie, chilihead zero. He—I'm assuming a "he," though it certainly might have been a "she"; in any event she or he was probably an adolescent, owing to the not insignificant amount of reckless jackassery necessary for this sort of operation—watches a buddy pick a little berry from a bush. It's small and colorful. It's even cute. The two teenagers—we'll call them Dorg and Crag—have seen birds eating the berries, so they figure said berries can't be too bad for them. Dorg pops one into his mouth and bites down. His eyes widen as he gapes at Crag with bewildered terror. He spits out the demon plant, but it's too late. His face reddens as he paces, clutching his cheeks and hair, sucking in cool air, and calling for water, which doesn't, once it arrives, help much. The fire in Dorg's mouth seems only to grow as tears pour involuntarily from his eye sockets and snot drips from his nostrils. Until finally, as if by magic, the fire disappears as mysteriously as it arrived, having burned nothing at all.

"Damn, Dorg. Pass me one of those," Crag says.

Crag is no coward. We can at least give him that.

The adventures of Dorg and Crag raise a question: Why would Crag say that? And more to the point (since you can envision some kind of idiotic dare scenario that might have forced both their hands on the first round) once both Dorg and Crag had eaten the demon berry, the episode raises a deeper, more interesting question: Why do it again?

What Dorg and Crag experienced was pain, an evolved sensation buried so deep in our cells, our selves, that it is inextricably linked with what it is to be an animal. Try spiritual exuberance, illegal drugs, the funniest joke you ever heard, and even orgasmic ecstasy, and I promise that for sheer clarity of the sensation and force of the moment none will compare to driving a nail through your foot. You can feel pain as a slap in the face or the slow degrading of your joints or the agony of lost love, and each will, to one degree or another, affect you at a level both physical and emotional, and perhaps even spiritual. We can feel pain at a depth and to a degree that we simply cannot feel pleasure—unless, of course, the pleasure is the pain, which points toward the essence of our story. You could say pain is where the body meets the soul.

Pain's reason for being is the simple, clear message it sends: whatever you're doing, *stop*. For the most part it works quite well. Try it once and you learn not to stick your hand in the fire. Poke the big mean guy enough times and he'll make sure you learn not to poke him again. We can turn pain into an abstraction to imagine potential future sources of pain, like falling from a cliff, getting stabbed by an enemy, or being hated by someone we love, and work to avoid them by walking carefully on a cliff side, having a bigger sword, or being nice. Pain is what keeps us alive.

But the picture is murkier than all that. Sometimes we inflict pain on ourselves. We watch movies that are scary or sad. We play violent contact sports. We dip gingerly into a steaming hot bath. In each of those scenarios there are aspects of the experience that are pleasurable in a different and more straightforward way, but the pain is an essential part of the pleasure too. Scary movies are not enjoyable despite their being scary—we watch them *because they scare us*. In my brief career as a high school rugby player I enjoyed many things about being on the field competing against other (almost always bigger, better) players, but I can assure you there's something exhilarating about the moment you crash into another person, something intrinsic to the pain that commands your full attention. A steaming hot bath may be good for the circulation, but isn't there a tinge of something else there, a purely sensual pleasure in forcing your body to indulge in the pain instead of leaping out of the tub, like tonguing a loose tooth or putting a little weight on a sprained ankle?

Some of us douse our food in hot sauce, and let there be no misunderstanding: hot sauce causes pain. You may enjoy any number of things about hot sauce, like the flavors, the way it looks drizzled over a plate, or just the knowledge that it's healthier than most condiments, but if you like hot sauce, you've also got to come to terms with the unifying factor, pain-inducing chemicals in chilies, and the fact that you like to inflict pain on yourself. If you've ever used hot sauce while cooking for friends or even, and perhaps especially, a love interest, you are, to at least some degree, a sadomasochist. It's time to embrace the kink.

Several years before embarking on this project I wrote a book about a major national security breach. The experience was emotionally and psychologically taxing, and as I searched for my next endeavor, I knew I didn't want to go down that road again, not yet at least. For years I'd kicked around an idea for a book about booze, but having just wrested myself with substantial effort from bad habits acquired during the fairly drenched decade of my twenties, I was in no mood. Many interesting things have been written and will yet be written on the subject of alcohol, but the act of drinking in itself is, in the end, not all that interesting. Do it a little and you get giddy, do it a lot and you get drunk, and there you have it.

It occurred to me, though, that there's something else widely popular that comes in a bottle. Its devotees talk about being addicted to it, and everyone seems to have a story about the time they over-indulged. The explanation for why it is so widely enjoyed is significantly more interesting than in the case of alcohol, and it has this peculiar characteristic that drink does not (not until the morning after, at least): it causes actual physical pain. Hot sauce.

With just a flicker of an idea at the time, I went to the NYC Hot Sauce Expo, then in its second year, where I tried a dollop of Grinders Death Nectar sauce. I've been a hot sauce lover since I was a kid, but let's not mince words: I'm a honky from eastern Oklahoma, and at the time this was by far the spiciest thing I'd ever had. I went, in a word, apeshit. After gumming a scoop of ice cream for a few minutes that felt like hours and finally harnessing my proverbial chi, I crawled back to the Grinders booth to enjoy the spectacle of others dosing themselves; sadism is half of sadomasochism, remember. I asked one woman who was clearly in serious pain what she thought. "It hurts, but I love it," she mumbled, laughing and crying as if at some kind of weird, hilarious funeral. There aren't many contexts in which her comment would make sense, and one of them, if described here, would land this book in an altogether more adult kind of bookstore.

As I dug further, I found that hot sauce sales in the United States are growing with extraordinary speed, far outpacing the market growth of other condiments, for reasons both fascinating and complex that speak to defining pieces of the American story. I learned that hot sauce has long held a special place in the hearts of billions and especially the world's poor because it's the people's condiment, affordable and tasty with a long shelf life.

While on a trip to California I stopped in at a small shop called Light My Fire at the Los Angeles Farmer's Market, where bottles of hot sauce line the walls floor to ceiling (not unlike bottles of liquor in their own kind of store, come to think of it). I'd never been to such a place, and I went full-on kid in a candy shop. Later at the airport I nearly became a TSA casualty when an agent asked if I had liquids in my bag. I forgot that the dozen-and-some-odd bottles of hot sauce sitting at the top of my bag were technically liquids. Only later did I learn that such stores exist from coast to coast. Ketchup, mayonnaise, mustard, and the rest may have their fans, but nowhere in the world of food does the passion of devotees and the ire of haters burn more brightly than in the case of sauces made of chilies. Growing sales, boutique shops, and new festivals—there was something happening here, and I needed to explore it.

We have become a nation obsessed with hot sauce. I wanted to know how that happened. Though today the United States is the indisputable headquarters of small-batch innovation in the world of hot sauce, such was not always the case. How, in a country cobbled together from English, French, and Spanish colonies—all land once controlled by Native Americans, none or very few of whom used chilies—did hot sauce become so popular? And more interestingly—since what we're talking about, after all, is a plant that induces pain, a sensation intended to repel us—*why?* These are the questions I set out to answer in these pages.

Now for a few logistical odds and ends.

When you decide to put pen to paper on anything related to the genus *Capsicum*, you are inevitably confronted—in the United States, at least—with the nagging issue of just what, exactly, this fruit is called. In New Mexico it's a chile. In much of the United States it's a pepper or a chili pepper. Sometimes it's even a chilli pepper. In much of the English-speaking world it's simply a chili.

In these pages I have tended to use the latter spelling, *chili*, because it is a widely accepted spelling in the language in which I write, because it comes closest to the original Mesoamerican word whence all other derivations come, and because the fact that the word *pepper* is there at all is the result of a big misunderstanding. At times for reasons of clarity or rhetorical whim I have used the term *chili pepper*. Other times I have kept to the spelling convention used by others, as in the title of an organization, like the Chile Pepper Institute in Las Cruces, New Mexico, for example. Suffice it to say that it will be made clear if I'm ever talking about black pepper rather than a chili.

And another thing.

Here's a conversation that happens many times over when you're writing a book about hot sauce.

"I'm writing a book about hot sauce."

"Oh yeah? Have you tried _____?" (Variation: "Have you been to _____?")

"No."

"Oh you can't write a book about hot sauce without trying _____!/visiting _____!"

Everyone has a favorite sauce and every country/state/city/ neighborhood has at least one unchallengeable claim to one thing or another. Much of the time it's a fair point and you probably shouldn't write about hot sauce without trying X or visiting Y. There is a world of amazing hot sauces and fascinating people who make them and love them.

Alas, while the world of hot sauce may appear limitless, the time and space to report and write about them are not. You have to stop somewhere. This book is not an encyclopedia of hot sauces, a taxonomy, or a collection of recipes. (There are a number of good books of that sort out there; I recommend anything by Dave DeWitt as a great place to start, in particular *The Hot Sauce Bible*, which is sort of the bible of the genre.) Nor is the purpose of this book to draw boundaries to determine what counts as hot sauce and what doesn't or to decide which hot sauce is best and which is worst.

Hot Sauce Nation is a journey in celebration of the most popular condiment on earth and a tribute to the people who make it and the people who love it. The book is about the people and places in the United States that can help us understand how and why hot sauce became so popular in America.

On my way to the airport at the end of that visit to Los Angeles, unknowingly headed toward a TSA smackdown with my bagful of hot sauce, I struck up a conversation with Karl, a driver with the rideshare service Lyft who was giving me a ride. We made small talk and briefly remarked on what a disaster it would be for me if the New York Knicks ever move to Denver. Then he asked what I was up to in L.A.

"Visiting friends. Exploring an idea," I said. "I found this shop here in town, Light My Fire. I'm thinking about writing a book about hot sauce."

Karl laughed. "No way," he said.

He seemed to channel the essence of California as he spoke, his easygoing diction almost singsongy, with the permanent hint of a smile.

"That's how I met my wife."

More on that in a moment. First we've got to eat our vegetables.

1

A BRIEF HISTORY OF HEAT

In 1491, the world was in many of its aspects and characteristics a minimum of two worlds—the New World, of the Americas, and the Old World, consisting of Eurasia and Africa. Columbus brought them together, and almost immediately and continually ever since, we have had an exchange of native plants, animals and diseases moving back and forth across the oceans between the two worlds. A great deal of the economic, social, political history of the world is involved in the exchange of living organisms between the two worlds.

—ALFRED W. CROSBY, JR.,
AUTHOR OF *THE COLUMBIAN EXCHANGE*

In the beginning, God created a man and named him Narama and a woman whom he named Uxuu. Narama and Uxuu lived in a land of plenty where they wanted for neither food nor sustenance. In time, God cast them from this Eden.

Having been evicted from his homeland, Narama began to sweat so profusely that he came to be covered in salt. The Creator was, at the time, busy giving jobs to the creatures of the earth—he's the keeper of this, she's the keeper of that, and so on. Uxuu, the first woman, was put in charge of the seeds and fruits of summer, and of rain. Narama, the first man, was given the enviable job of overseeing salt, mescal, and chili.

With roles assigned, the Creator invited everyone to a big potluck fiesta around a table situated on the center of the earth, to which all the creatures of creation brought their special foods. The last to arrive, Narama, showed up naked and covered in salt—patron saint of mescal, remember. With everyone seated around the table, Narama scraped salt from his face and sprinkled it on the food. He then grabbed his testicles, which turned into chili pods, plucked them, and began sprinkling his fiery new spice onto the fare.

This went over with the other guests about as well as one might expect. Around the table creatures shouted in protest and scolded Narama for defiling dinner. He asked that they give him a chance. If everyone else got to contribute their thing, shouldn't he be able to add his own specialty to the buffet? Just try it and you'll see, he pleaded, that there's nothing better for a good meal than salt and chili.

Brave souls that they were, the others gave Narama's chili testes a shot. They ate, it burned, and they loved it. And thus, from the scrotum of the patron saint of mescal, who showed up late to a party naked and covered in salt, the first creatures on earth were converted into the world's original chiliheads.

The above comes from the creation mythology of the Cora, a people indigenous to central-western Mexico who still speak a language related to the Nahuatl tongue spoken by the Aztec. It's not incidental that Narama was the patron saint of both chili and salt, the only spice that is not a plant but a mineral essential for human survival (or, for that matter, the patron saint of mescal, but that's another story). In preindustrial societies salt was a rock on which empires were built and crushed, and the quest for it a matter of life and death. Let the fact that the saint who spoke for salt also spoke for chili speak for itself.

The Cora creation story is a particularly colorful one, but it is far from unique. Indigenous cultures throughout the Americas celebrate and revere the chili as a food, a medicine, and a sacrament central to their place in the cosmos. The Inca believed the chili was one of the four original gods and the brother of the first Inca king. The Maya prescribed chilies to treat a cough and a sore throat. The Aztec used an early form of pepper spray as kind of primitive chemical warfare by burning huge amounts of chili upwind from their enemies. Like many cultures after them, the Aztec punished errant children by making them eat a spicy chili pepper. They also dropped a little chili juice on a tooth to soothe its aching. The Aztec, and other civilizations, held the plant so sacred that abstinence from chili and sex was an important form of religious fasting.

Scientists believe the chili plant most likely emerged out of the evolutionary soup in a small area in Bolivia north of Sucre that straddles the Río Grande, a river that flows easterly into the Mamoré and ultimately the Amazon. Bolivians today enthusiastically eat the *ulupica* chili, a mostly wild variety that closely resembles members of that original pioneer community. These, or the similar but domesticated *locoto* pepper, are the spicy ingredient in a simple sauce made of chilies, tomatoes, and sometimes a little salt known as *llajwa*. Because of the geographic and genetic proximity of the ingredients and people who make llajwa to the ingredients and people who lived in the area in prehistory, it may well be that llajwa was—ready for it?—the world's first hot sauce.

On the other hand, the earliest evidence we have of humans bold enough to chow down on chili peppers comes from excavations of a group of cave dwellings in southern Mexico led by archaeologist Richard Stockton MacNeish in the 1960s. Those digs turned up evidence dating to as early as about 6000 BCE of elaborate burials, including one of a child with its skull smashed in—in his report MacNeish suspects there may have been "some sort of dirty work afoot . . . perhaps evidence of human sacrifice?"—as well as evidence of squash and chilies in the remains of discarded vegetable matter and, in case you needed proof that these people were actually chewing and swallowing the chilies, in *caprolites*, the polite term for the fossilized poop.

The earliest known word for a chili pepper is in the Proto-Oto-Manguean language spoken in roughly the same region of southern Mexico as far back as 6,500 or more years ago. The word, rendered as *ʔki3 in the International Phonetic Alphabet, is a hypothetical reconstruction of a word that no longer exists in a language that has gone extinct, so it's impossible to say for sure how exactly the oldest known word for the chili sounded coming out of the mouths of prehistoric Proto-Oto-Manguean speakers. But linguistic anthropologist Dr. Cecil Brown, who led a study on the subject, points us in the right direction. "I guess that the closest English word to the Proto-Oto-Manguean word for chili peppers," Brown told me, "is *key*."

The word *chili* comes to English by way of Mexican Spanish from the Aztec language Nahuatl, and it's not alone. In addition to *chili*, English also inherited from Nahuatl the words *chocolate, mesquite, avocado, sapodilla, tomato, peyote*, and, for what it's worth, *shack*.

As with many crops, exactly when and where wild chili pepper plants were domesticated is difficult to determine, largely because domestication is more a gradual process than a revolution. Small hunter-gatherer bands might cull and nurture a group of wild plants, or transplant a few closer to camp, well before larger villages start plowing and harvesting fields. But it's certainly plausible—indeed, it seems only logical—that humans were eating wild chilies before they started farming them.

"We know from the paleobiolinguistic evidence that people were interested in chili peppers in some parts of the Americas at least one thousand years before (in the case of Oto-Manguean at least three thousand years earlier than) the development of village farming," says Dr. Brown. "Whether this interest involved domesticated or wild peppers is difficult to determine."

What we are reasonably sure of is that people started cultivating different varieties of chilies independently of one another in different parts of Latin America.

It's a truism that taxonomic classification is an inexact science at best—in its unrelenting indifference nature recognizes no species or genus, only the spectrum of life in its myriad forms—but that fact has never been more evident than in the case of chili peppers.

All chilies belong to the genus *Capsicum*, a word that comes to us from Joseph Pitton de Tournefort, the seventeenth-century French botanist at the royal garden of Louis XIV and a forebear of modern taxonomy, whose posthumously published *Institutiones rei herbaria* contains the first description of the genus. Why Tournefort assigned chilies the moniker remains a matter of speculation, but it's generally believed that he named it for either the Latin *capsa*, meaning "box"— a reference to the generally hollow interior of a chili pepper—or the Greek *kapto*, meaning "to bite," in reference to the obvious. Debate over the precise boundaries of and within the genus *Capsicum* has been simmering ever since.

Of the twenty-five or so known species of chili, just five (or four, or three, depending on how you slice it) have been domesticated, and within each are numerous cultivars, varieties of the species further refined through cultivation.

Capsicum pubescens, so named because of its hairy leaves, is found almost exclusively in midelevation areas running along the Andes mountains from Colombia to northern Chile. This is the locoto pepper used today in the ancient Bolivian llajwa hot sauce and a close relative of the wild ulupica peppers that most resemble the ancestral crew.

Capsicum baccatum is a variety found primarily in a wide band across South America, with a great many cultivars ranging from hot to mild, like the South American *aji* and the bishop's hat, so named because of its bizarre flattened-cone shape.

The following three are closely related, and there is ongoing debate within the taxonomic community as to where, precisely, lie the lines between species. We won't wade into that debate.

Capsicum chinense is not a Chinese pepper but a Brazilian one, originating in the Amazon and endemic in pre-Columbian times to a wide swath of northern South America, Central America, and the Caribbean. Cultivars include some of the hottest peppers on earth, such as the habanero, Scotch bonnet, Carolina reaper, and Bhut Jolokia, also known as the ghost pepper.

Capsicum frutescens is both widely used and not. Few of its cultivars are grown in any significant quantities except the Peri Peri pepper in Africa and the big one, tabasco, used in the eponymous sauce.

Capsicum annuum—yet another naming foible, since in the absence of frost this species is not an annual but a perennial—is by far the most widely grown species. Its cultivars include the bell pepper, ancho, jalapeño, serrano, cayenne, and many others.

Now for a word on pepper.

On a day in late April 1493, down the crowded, crooked streets of medieval Barcelona, in the vaulted banquet hall of the Grand Royal Palace, Christopher Columbus bowed before Queen Isabella of

Castile and King Ferdinand of Aragon, and—we must assume—took a deep and uneasy breath to steady his quivering heart.

The Genoese navigator had just returned from a voyage around the world to the east end of Asia and back. The expensive trip had been largely funded by the monarchs before him, and he'd brought back an odd and somewhat disappointing assortment of souvenirs: six unquestionably terrified Indians, two parrots (green and yellow), a regrettably small amount of gold, and some cinnamon, which did not, all agreed, taste right. Missing from Columbus's assortment of proofs that he'd made the journey was an item the Italian merchant Marco Polo had brought back to much acclaim from his own trip to Asia via the overland eastern route two centuries earlier: black pepper. Indeed, Columbus had been partly inspired by Polo to make his journey and had taken with him a heavily annotated copy of the account of Polo's travels. Finding a better and cheaper way to get to pepper was sort of the whole point of getting to the Far East by sailing west in the first place.

Though always exotic, for the European upper classes spices were more or less readily available in the world of antiquity, when traders along the rim of the Indian Ocean from East Asia to Arabia maintained a robust mercantile network that connected the Far East to the Mediterranean and beyond. Records survive of Roman sentries using pepper to season their meals while keeping tense watch against Caledonian barbarians at Hadrian's Wall in the far north of modern-day England. Notwithstanding the occasional hiccup, throughout the Middle Ages, trade between Europe and the East continued such that a taste for spices among Europeans steadily grew. In time, even people outside the upper gentry could occasionally afford to enliven their food with exotic Oriental spices. Pepper was the most prized spice of all.

It's difficult for moderns to comprehend the place pepper held in the European minds of the distant past. Spices came from farther away than nearly any European had ever traveled, and they were, on the whole, outrageously expensive, marked up by middlemen on the long trade routes from their distant places of origin. The name given by Europeans to the Spice Islands was, in its time, a literal description of a place shrouded in myth and mystery whence came some of the most prized commodities known to humankind. Every clove consumed on earth came from a string of five tiny volcanic islands in eastern Indonesia. All nutmeg came from a similarly minuscule archipelago not far to the south. The world's pepper came from the jungles of southern India and out through the Malabar Coast on the southwestern tip of the subcontinent.

In a world with virtually no long-distance communication or reliable maps, when rumor, fantasy, and terror slathered together in the mind to paint a fearsome mirage of the world beyond the small confines of one's own immediate experience, spices were precious and tangible artifacts from alien lands—specifically the Orient, with its fabled harems, infidels, and exotic seductions. Many believed spices possessed powerful medicinal, psychoactive, and sometimes dangerous properties, especially as aphrodisiacs. Pepper in particular was looked on as a treacherous narcotic capable of awakening over-powering lust—or sexual prowess, depending on one's point of view.

Take, for example, a tale from the extraordinary life of Duke William IX of Aquitaine, a lyric poet and early troubadour who, as author Jack Turner puts it in his essential *Spice: The History of a Temptation*, "on account of his riotous living" managed to both lead a minor Crusade and be excommunicated by the Vatican. Twice.

In a poem that professes to recount a not altogether unflatter-ing misadventure—today we might call his tale a "humblebrag"—William tells of a summer's day when, riding through Auvergne, in modern-day France, he was abducted by two noble ladies who imprisoned him in their castle and put him to use for a week of steamy ménage à trois. William confesses that before regaining his freedom he went 188 rounds, aided by a meal of two fat chickens, bread, wine, "and the pepper laid on thick."

"I nearly broke my tool and burst my harness," William laments. "I can't express the remorse that overtook me."

I'm sure.

To the medieval European, educated by folk wisdom and interpretations of the Bible handed down by church authorities, spices were of such enchanting potency that they were believed by many to originate, literally, from an earthly Paradise on the order of Adam and Eve's Eden. Where precisely Paradise lay was a matter of much speculation. The French crusader and medieval chronicler Jean de Joinville placed it at the headwaters of the Nile. Many understandably suspected terrestrial Paradise to be in the vicinity of the Spice Islands, and searching for them was no small matter, particularly with the vital established trade routes under the control of heathens. In 1453 Ottoman Turks sacked and claimed for themselves the Byzantine city of Constantinople, a mercantile bottleneck thereafter known to the world as Istanbul. With Turkish hands now wrapped firmly around trade routes from the East to the doorstep of Europe, prices for spices, and particularly pepper, soared. Finding a faster path to the heaven on earth whence came the world's exotic spices was suddenly a matter of the highest importance.

Thus, as Turner writes of Columbus's first voyage in 1492, "When he sailed west, he quite genuinely believed he was sailing to Paradise."

Pepper was absent from the gifts Columbus brought back from his voyage, of course, because he had not gone to Asia at all. The Indians were not Indians, but Ciguayo natives from what is now the Dominican Republic. The parrots were real (Caribbean, not Asian), but the cinnamon was just the bark of a tree that, in his obsessive yearning to reach the land of spices and earthly Paradise, Columbus convinced himself tasted something kind of like super-low-grade cinnamon. The gold was real gold, and over time it became the focus of many later journeys to the New World, but Columbus did not find any pepper, because pepper did not grow in the Americas. What he did find transformed life on earth more than all the pepper in India and the gold of El Dorado ever could: chili.

At two o'clock in the morning on October 11, 1492, on a night lit bright by a half moon, a sailor aboard the *Pinta* was the first of Columbus's crew to sight land. The admiral waited until the next day to come ashore, where he reported encountering a number of hearty, intelligent, and warmhearted people who, he recorded cryptically in his journal, would make good Christians and excellent servants. With presumably bemused natives looking on, the Europeans made their requisite declarations and affirmations laying claim to this land for the Holy Trinity, the King and Queen, and so on.

It may be that the people Columbus encountered—Lucayans living on an island in the Bahamas they called Guanahani—were more clever than merely kindhearted. When Columbus inquired whether they knew where to find gold, they gave an enthusiastic yes; there was a great king with heaps of it just a ways to the south, they said—away from here, anyway. Columbus invited them to show him the way, but they politely declined.

This became a pattern. On the evening of November 5, a small contingent Columbus had sent into the interior of one island returned to tell of finding another group of most-welcoming villagers. The Spaniards showed them specimens of pepper, which their hosts said they recognized—which is virtually impossible—and that there was plenty of the stuff, just not here; there was some a ways to the south-east, though, they said.

By mid-January, Columbus's tour of the Caribbean was becoming a tense affair. His ships were beginning to take on water, and morale among his crew ran low. Days earlier they'd had their first violent confrontation with a group islanders, and Columbus feared for the safety of the crew from the wrecked ship the *Santa María*, whom he'd left at a small fortress called La Navidad.

On January 15, 1493, in one of his final forays into the islands he'd bumped into on his way to India, Columbus wrote in his journal of encountering a plant growing wild that the natives called *aji*.

"The land was found to produce much *aji*, which is the pepper of the inhabitants, and more valuable than the common sort; they deem it very wholesome and eat nothing without it. Fifty caravels might be loaded every year with this commodity," he writes. The next day, Columbus with his two remaining ships set sail for Spain.

The *aji* was obviously something far stranger than the black pepper to which Spaniards had become accustomed, so Columbus took a few samples of it to show the folks at home. One court regular in Spain who tasted aji said it was twenty times hotter than the usual stuff. This was an understatement if ever there was one, because black pepper, lacking entirely in the chemical that gives the chili pepper its bite, is not spicy at all.

Columbus's misidentification of the chili as pepper has been a source of much confusion ever since. Though in broad strokes they may have some similarities—it's fair to say that the two are both pungent—black pepper and the chili are chemically and botanically distinct.

Piper nigrum, the scientific name for black pepper, is a vine under the taxonomic family Piperacaea that grows natively in the jungles of southern India. Incidentally, pepper's own name is also the result of a case of mistaken identity; the word *pepper* is a derivative of the Tamil word *pippali*, which, according to Jean Andrews's *Peppers: The Domesticated Capsicums*, was the word for "the fruit of the sacred fig tree," affixed by Indians to varieties of pepper either because of a shared religious significance or simply because the two look alike.

Chilies, on the other hand, fall under the taxonomic family Solanaceae, or nightshade, which includes other important crops like tomatoes and potatoes. Many plants in the family (for example, tobacco) contain alkaloids, chemical compounds that are often poisonous and/or psychoactive in humans, such as nicotine, caffeine, morphine, cocaine, and the most widely used and abused of them all, found only in the chili pepper: capsaicin.

Chili peppers have unique tastes and aromas across a wide spectrum, owing to varying combinations of hundreds of different chemical compounds. The main compound, though, is called alkyl-methoxypyrazine, the most readily sensed molecular variation of which, 3-isobutal-2-methoxypyrazine, is that classic bell pepper taste. You'll note that this chemical can't account for what we love most in chilies because bell peppers aren't spicy.

What bell peppers lack, rare among the *Capsicum* genus, is an odorless, tasteless, crystalline chemical compound known as capsaicin, which lives most concentratedly in the chili pepper's placenta. By stimulating nerve endings in the mouth and skin, capsaicin triggers the production of a neurotransmitter called substance P, which signals to the brain that the body is in pain, specifically because it is on fire. The same reaction takes place when the nerves come in contact with heat above 109 degrees Fahrenheit. Capsaicin is nearly insoluble in water, which is why a glass of H_2O doesn't do much good in battle with an overdose of Dave's Insanity Sauce. Thanks to a fortuitous result of plant evolution, capsaicin is soluble in fat and alcohol, so a nice big scoop of ice cream or a beer will often help, though the carbonation in the latter tends to add to the irritation.

The pungency of a chili pepper—its concentration of capsaicin—is traditionally measured in Scoville heat units (SHU), named for the American pharmacist Wilbur Lincoln Scoville, who devised the Scoville Organoleptic Test at a Detroit-based pharmaceutical company in 1912. The test measures the degree to which a chili pepper solution must be diluted before capsaicin is no longer detectable to a professional taster. Nowadays a less subjective test, High-Performance Liquid Chromatography, is used to analyze capsaicin content, but heat is still generally described in SHU. With the bell pepper weighing in at 0 SHU, Cholula hot sauce clocks about 1,000 SHU. Tabasco Pepper Sauce comes up to around 5,000 SHU. Grinders Death Nectar out of Kansas City burns at 337,000 SHU. It goes up from there. Pure capsaicin tops out the Scoville scale at 16,000,000 SHU.

But as any astute chili eater knows from experience, the mere "spiciness" of a chili doesn't tell the whole story. Some chilies come on fast, while some come on slow. Some strike and vanish, while others linger. In fact, capsaicin is just one of at least twenty-two compounds, called capsaicinoids, that account for a pepper's heat in the myriad forms it takes. The true spiciness of a chili is not a two-dimensional spectrum but, as Dr. Paul Bosland, director of the Chile Pepper Institute in Las Cruces, New Mexico, clarified for me, an intricate dance of different yet related sensations.

"A couple decades ago I had a student from Guatemala who said the *rocoto** or *manazano*, the *Capsicum pubescens*, was hotter than the habanero," he said. But when the institute ran its standard capsaicin

---

* Same as the locoto used in llajwa hot sauce in Bolivia, this chili goes under many names in different regions. They're all the same hairy little *Capsicum pubescens*, though.

test, the rocoto came nowhere near the habanero in its concentration of capsaicinoids. "We noticed they had a lot of those minor capsaicinoids, what we would call rare capsaicinoids," Dr. Bosland said. "Those minor capsaicinoids give kind of a lingering heat—and in humans if the heat keeps lingering and lingering, we always say it's hotter than if it dissipates quickly."

Outside the door to his office at New Mexico State University, in the slot where most people identify themselves as the Dean of this or the Director of that or what have you, Bosland simply calls himself "Chileman." If anyone, he'd know.

Dr. Bosland developed a multidimensional heat profile to more fully describe a chili pepper's heat, including five separate descriptors: how fast or delayed the heat is (Asian chilies tend to come on fast, while habaneros come on slowly); how long it lingers (habaneros stick around, but jalapeños dissipate more quickly); the sharpness or flatness of the heat (cayennes are sharper, like pins sticking in the mouth, whereas New Mexican chilies are flatter, like the heat is applied with a paintbrush); where the heat is strongest (jalapeños burn nearer the tongue and lips, habaneros attack the back of the throat); and finally how much heat the chili has. These are our good old-fashioned SHU.

There's at least one striking difference between wild and domesticated chilies, and it may help us understand why capsaicinoids exist at all: wild peppers tend to grow erect, pointed toward the sky, while domesticated varieties tend to grow pendant, hanging toward the ground. Though capsaicin causes a wicked burning sensation in mammals—and thank goodness for that—it has no such effect on the birds that chilies depend on to spread their seeds. The mammalian digestive process destroys the chili seed's ability to reproduce, but the seeds pass through a bird's guts unharmed—capsaicin may have evolved as a way to scare off mammals while leaving chili peppers for the birds. Wild chilies evolved to grow erect as a further enticement to birds, which then spread the seeds far and wide. Domesticated varieties grow hanging down because they've been selected to be bigger and heavier and they have no need for avian assistance to reproduce.

But scaring off mammals isn't capsaicin's entire reason for being; it has useful antimicrobial properties. In controlled studies of wild chili populations, scientists have found that plants with higher exposure to deadly fungus are spicier, indicating that they may produce more capsaicin to fight off infection. Capsaicin also acts as an insecticide, warding off potentially harmful pests. Humanity's favorite drug likely also evolved as a part of a plant's immune system.

Contrary to what many people in the throes of a hot sauce overdose infer, capsaicin is not corrosive—the burning sensation is an illusion. You can clean anything copper with hot sauce (works wonders on copper kitchenware), but that's an effect of its acidity, primarily of the vinegar. As a result, hot sauce does have some industrial applications. John Barna, president of Modern Tool & Manufacturing, sometimes uses hot sauce—Frank's RedHot, in this case—to clean copper on small jobs. Typically he uses chromate conversion coating for the task, but, he told me, "It's very volatile. The hot sauce, environmentally speaking, takes the edge off. It doesn't get it squeaky clean, but take a dirty penny and soak it in it, and you'll see what I'm talking about." (It cleans the penny.)

The one mammal capsaicin has failed to scare away is the human, and there's strong evidence to suggest that, in addition to the fact that they're just delicious, we may have started eating and cultivating chilies for their medicinal and antimicrobial properties. Fresh chilies are packed with nutrients like folic acid, potassium, and vitamins A, E, and about six times as much vitamin C as found in an orange. Like salt and smoke, chilies also help slow down spoilage in food—not unimportant in an age before refrigeration, particularly in tropical regions, where ice simply did not exist. In instance after instance, researchers find the ubiquity of chilies in the gastro-medicinal practices of native peoples in the Americas. The Maya not only ate virtually all food with some amount of chili but also prescribed it as a medicine for diverse ailments, including earaches, bowel troubles, and respiratory problems. Dr. Francisco Hernández, physician to King Felipe II of Spain and the first European to systematically collect plants in the Americas, who lived in Mexico from 1570 to 1577, reports that among the natives chilies were known to produce all manner of digestive emollients, from eased bowel movements to farts. Today we know this to be true because chilies increase the production of stomach acids in the digestive tract.

Even the most exotic old-world spices had millennia to spread and become familiar, if only in the faintest way or to the most elite, to people throughout Africa, Europe, and Asia. And taken altogether there were few spices introduced from the New World to the Old; in addition to capsicum, the Americas' only noteworthy contributions to the spice cabinet were vanilla and allspice. Thus when chilies hit European shores in the fifteenth century, something unprecedented happened to world cuisine. It's fair to say that chilies were the first spice to go viral.

Chilies were in Spain with Columbus's return in 1493. As the Portuguese made their way to Asia, they introduced chilies to Africa, India, and the Far East. The marauding Ottomans brought chili peppers to the Balkans in the sixteenth century, from where they made their way north to become the paprika Hungarians cherish as a cornerstone of their national cuisine. Chilies were present in Italy— mercifully for lovers of pepperoni—no later than 1535. Around the same time, chilies made their way to the Germans, who thought they'd originated in India and thus called them Calicut peppers, a common and resilient misconception.

Even today, people often profess disbelief when presented with the fact that chilies are native only to the Americas, that when Columbus set sail for India in 1492, Indian food was not spicy.

To reiterate, lest the point is lost: before 1493 no food outside the Western Hemisphere contained any trace of capsaicin, which is to say that the sensation of "spicy"—in the sense that we most often mean it, as the burning sensation that capsaicin simulates—did not exist in the Old World. Thai food was not spicy. Neither were the cuisines of Calabria, Hungary, Senegal, Ethiopia, Malaysia, or Tunisia. Sichuan food may have given a tingling sensation, owing to the use of Sichuan peppercorns, which are unrelated to chilies, but neither it nor any other dish in the whole of China was spicy in the way of chilies.

When Europeans first encountered them at the end of the fifteenth century, chilies were unknown to anyone outside of the Americas. Today the chili is perhaps the most widely grown spice on earth, and by extension hot sauce in its myriad forms is humanity's favorite condiment.

A visit to the spiritual heartland of hot sauce . . .

The road from sea level on Mexico's Pacific coast nearly twirls as it swerves its way along cliffs of the Sierra Madre and up and down a seemingly endless series of switchbacks through extremely rugged terrain, until finally settling at 5,200 feet in the Valley of Oaxaca. From the coastal town of Puerto Escondido the fastest route overland takes about seven hours* on a potholed road that

---

* A highway project under way in 2015 was poised to cut the trip to just three hours.

periodically dips through small communities. It's easy to envision just how isolated such places would have been in antiquity and even in the not-so-distant past.

More indigenous people live in Oaxaca than any other state in Mexico, and over half the population of this largely rural and poor state speaks a non-Spanish native language, generally of the Oto-Manguean family (descendant of the Proto-Oto-Manguean, which gave us our oldest known word for chili, the one pronounced something like "key"). Owing both to the depth of its indigenous roots and to the isolation imposed on communities by the region's uneven geography, Oaxaca is rightly revered for the richness of its cultural diversity, particularly as it pertains to cuisine. The state has a nickname: Land of Seven Moles. Oaxaca's eponymous capital is an old city planned and maintained in the Spanish colonial style, with plazas and imposing churches, built compact along straight but narrow streets, many of them paved in stone. It's the region's commercial and cultural hub.

Armando Ruiz sat across from me at a workshop table in his art studio on the north side of downtown Oaxaca.

"The artistic thing is special here," he said. "Everyone paints or cooks." We were surrounded on all sides by sculptures and paintings, many of them unfinished. Earthy colors. Skulls. I asked Armando for his earliest memory of chili.

"You never think of it," he said, followed by a universal truth: "You just remember the times when it really gets you." His family comes from an area called Villa Alta about five hours into the mountains north of town. He told me an old family story about an uncle who as a child developed a strange fixation with licking one spot on the side of his family's adobe home. Armando's grandmother patched the spot with adobe mixed with a chili paste to keep the kid away. It worked.

Armando is part Zapotec (a major indigenous group in the region), but he was born and grew up in Mexico City before moving to Oaxaca fourteen years ago. "I have always been connected to Oaxaca," he said. "It's always like that. If you are from Oaxaca, you are always going to be influenced by it, even if you leave, because there is a unifying force in the culture." He has the diaspora's nostalgic love for the homeland, and in Oaxaca he's come home. When I asked where to go for typical Oaxacan food he didn't hesitate with his response.

Several blocks from Armando's studio, El Escapulario is a simply appointed restaurant up an unremarkable staircase on the corner of Calle de Manuel García Vigil and Quetzalcoatl. Esther Leonor Alonso García has lived in Oaxaca for forty years and opened El Escapulario more than a decade ago after honing her cooking craft first with her grandmother and mother, then in kitchens around Oaxaca. She grew up near the town of Pochutla, inland from the Pacific coast in the foothills of the Sierra Madre.

I sat at a table with Esther and ordered, more or less at random, a massive meal of chicken breast, in a dark sauce of *pasilla* chilies, oil, garlic, onions, and *chapulines* (grasshoppers), and a *tlayuda*, sometimes aptly called a Mexican pizza, covered in Oaxacan beef, spicy pork, chorizo, *quesillo* (a special sort of Oaxacan cheese), and chapulines, with a hot sauce on the side of pasilla chilies, tomato, garlic, onion, and chapulines. Such is the cuisine of Oaxaca that one can by happenstance order a three-part meal unified by a grasshopper theme.

We talked about her childhood and a simple sauce ever present on her family table made of *tusta* chilies, which grow in Oaxaca's coastal region, tomato, and *chicatanas* (flying ants). Then we turned to mole.

The word *mole* is believed to derive from the Nahuatl *molli*, meaning "mixture" (*guaca* is Nahuatl for "vegetable," so . . .). The dish most Americans think of when hearing the word *mole* is just one variety, mole poblano (or *mole negro*), a thick, dark, and earthy sauce made with a multitude of spices, chilies, and lots of dark chocolate. In addition to mole negro, in Oaxaca, the Land of Seven Moles, you'll find *mole rojo*, with more chilies, less chocolate, plus almonds and peanuts. There's also *coloradito, amarillo, verde, chichilo,* and *manchamantel.* Each is a unique choreography of ingredients from the region and around the world, like cinnamon, black pepper, cloves, and many, many more. As is to be expected on questions of food, it's disputed whether there are really seven moles. Esther, for instance, says there are more like four that really fit the definition. On the other hand, each family will have its own twist on a recipe, so who's to say there aren't hundreds of different moles? Thousands?

In any case, mole is an element of Oaxacan cuisine that is rich in both taste and the culture that envelops it. Properly done from market to table, a mole, Esther told me, takes three or four days to make. "I think it's a fundamental thing for us," she said, as I shoveled heaping piles of chorizo and grasshoppers drizzled with grasshopper sauce into my mouth. "We use it for our funerals, weddings, baptisms, all special occasions in all towns. It's the traditional Oaxacan food that stands out."

As a bedrock on which many a meal is prepared, mole is not a condiment and thus not a hot sauce of the sort we're exploring. But it's an early evolutionary progenitor, like the creatures recorded in fossils of primitive primates that begin to suggest shoulders pulling back and hips narrowing as our species slowly began to stand upright.

When we look for those peculiar traits that mark us and bind us together as uniquely human, few endeavors shine as brightly as art and cooking, and especially cooking with artistry. As a complex dish that takes days to prepare, and which anchors ritual meals from birth to grave, mole combines the two. And though chilies are ever present in mole and chocolate is a frequent ingredient, all moles are enlivened with additional spices, sometimes dozens, nearly all of them from the Old World. Mole is the first great sauce story of the Columbian Exchange, when, as with jazz, elements of the Old World and the New fused into something novel and funky, a never-before-seen culinary foundation on which to riff. Old meets new, and the thrill of capsaicin is invited into a carnival of other spices and preparations. Mole is the spiritual ancestor of hot sauce.

Uncountable delicious foods emerged from the meeting of those two worlds—take pizza, for instance, or poutine—but the spicy factor takes hot sauce into a world all its own. Some of us crave hot sauce, which can act on the brain in ways that mimic narcotics. What the Mexicans are after with mole, what we're all after with hot sauce, is something more than mere calories or nutrients, or even a delicious meal; we're after something spicier, hotter, jazzier, something beyond taste—something, if you'll allow me the indulgence, transcendent.

2

SOME LIKE IT HOT

Your heart sweats, your body shakes
Another kiss is what it takes
You can't sleep, you can't eat
There's no doubt, you're in deep
Your throat is tight, you can't breathe
Another kiss is all you need
—ROBERT PALMER, "ADDICTED TO LOVE"

There's a dent in the floor at Alaska Studio. Founded in 1977 by Pat Collier of the Vibrators, the legendary rehearsal and recording space in central London has hosted its share of riotous acts, like the Damned, the Cure, R.E.M., and the Jesus and Mary Chain. Among them was the post-punk/neo-folk group Death in June, which recorded a music video in Alaska's Studio #4, during the making of which a shotgun was discharged into the floor. Hence the dent.

Karl Leiker started working as a production engineer at Alaska Studio in the mid-1980s. He'd grown up in the San Francisco Bay Area, in a town south of Oakland called San Lorenzo, where he started playing the bass. From there he moved to Los Angeles, started gigging and auditioning, and in time linked together a series of semirandom connections, as one does when one is a bassist in one's twenties in Southern California, that landed him in London.

Karl immersed himself in the London music scene, playing in little bands, hanging out with promoters, and going to shows. Except for the lack of good Mexican food and the jalapeños he'd grown up with, London suited him. For a while he dated "a crazy French girl," he told me ("I ended up in trash bins because of this chick"), but after three years that torrid relationship ended and he was happily single, young, and rock 'n' roll. He started noticing a young woman at his gigs with blonde hair and blue eyes.

Late one rainy evening while waiting on a cab to shuttle him from one gig to yet another gig the same night, Karl noticed the blonde again. She was standing beside him outside the club, eating a piece of carrot cake she'd picked up at a late-night shop nearby. Karl looked at the blonde, then at the carrot cake, then leaned in and took a bite.

"Cheeky wanker!'" the blonde said. This was Helen.

Helen worked in the accounts and payroll department at Lloyd's Bank on the Isle of Dogs, an oxbow in the River Thames at London's East End. She loved music and collected 45s—bands like Dinosaur Jr., Killdozer, and Archers of Loaf. In her school days she listened to the BBC's legendary DJ John Peel and methodically wrote down the artist and song title of every track played during his set. She was half British and half Turkish and in the summer often took a road trip with her family from England back to Turkey. When she and Karl met, Helen was also recently out of her own long-term relationship.

Karl and Helen had mutual friends, and after the carrot cake incident they talked and joked around together when they'd see each other at shows. That evolved into an outing for pizza one night in Soho, just the two of them. Karl watched as Helen sprinkled heaps of chili flakes on her pizza slice. Here it is, he thought, common ground.

With their shared love of spicy food they embarked on an odyssey through London's multiethnic culinary scene searching for ever spicier meals. They were taken with each other. A favorite spot was Bintang, a mom-and-pop restaurant in Camden Town, in north London, specializing in pan-Asian cuisine with an emphasis in Malaysian fare and a vast selection of spicy chili sauces. They sunk into one another and their love for hot sauces, eating together and sharing the spectacle of reddened faces, snotty nostrils, giggle fits, and mouths on fire. They built their love on the bond of hot sauce.

"It's like, that's part of the reason we fell in love, if you know what I mean," Karl said. "It was kind of a common denominator, you know?" They were, as Karl told me, like one person with two heads, tied at the hip.

In 1997, Karl and Helen moved together to Los Angeles, where they became known among their friends as "that couple," the hot sauce fanatics. They threw dinner parties where they experimented with different combinations of varied chilies, Anaheims, habaneros, and pasillas. Dave's Insanity Sauce was a favorite bottled hot sauce. They'd heard once on a BBC science program that hugging and laughing helped people recover from a common cold faster, and they knew from experience that chilies help too.* "Helen and I would constantly tell folks 'hugging, laughing, and chilies' are good for you!" Karl told me.

They drew their friends and their relationship ever further into the arms of hot sauce with increasingly spicy food and the heady rush that accompanies a heavy dose of capsaicin.

---

* Studies show that capsaicin significantly helps reduce nasal congestion and sinus pressure. Incidentally, wasabi—the horseradish-like green goop that comes on a plate next to a sushi roll—inflames the nasal passages, creating the illusion that the congestion is cleared up when in fact it has no such effect.

"It's like—I'm gonna get deep with you on this—but it's like an orgasm," Karl told me. "And it's like taking some hard drugs to knock you out. I don't know if you've ever had any kind of surgery and had morphine or whatever, but it hits the same thing, you know?" The joke was that one of these days Karl and Helen were going to have to get straightened out at chilihab.

It's not an accident that hot sauce played such a central role in Karl and Helen falling in love. Sure, spicy food is common ground and the search for hot sauce a shared ritual and a journey to be taken together, but while they were laughing into each other's teary eyes over plates of vindaloo and curry mee, brain chemistry was working double time in the background.

In the exhilarating early stages of their relationship, their brains were releasing a naturally occurring neurochemical called phenylethylamine, a stimulant similar to amphetamine. This event triggers the release of norepinephrine, which causes the heightened awareness, sweaty palms, and pounding heart you'll remember from every time you've ever fallen in love. The same event also triggers the release of dopamine, a powerful brain chemical associated with the feeling of being rewarded and feeling pleasure. Cocaine and heroin work in different ways to increase the effects of dopamine, which gives the user both the intense pleasure associated with those drugs and the underlying reward sensation that reinforces the desire for more, leading to addiction. English rocker Robert Palmer was not totally off base when he sang in the chorus to his 1985 hit, "Might as well face it, you're addicted to love."

When capsaicin in hot sauce triggers the release of the pain-signaling neurotransmitter substance P under the illusion that the mouth is burning, the brain responds by releasing a flood of dopamine. The effect is not unlike a modulated form of the euphoria that comes from hard narcotics. A warm wave of pleasure washes over the psyche, and the brain whispers to itself that this is a reward, which may help explain part of the mystery of the pain/pleasure conundrum. And while each of the young lovers' brains was producing norepinephrine, capsaicin only added to its effects—sweat, delighted agitation, racing hearts. Dopamine in turn triggers the release of "the cuddle hormone," oxytocin, which our brains also release when we kiss and caress one another. Oxytocin lowers anxiety and strengthens bonds between people. Production of oxytocin in the brain surges during sex. Like an orgasm indeed, Karl.

There's an episode of *The Simpsons* famous among chiliheads in which Homer eats several of the "Merciless Peppers of Quetzlzacatenango, grown," Chief Wiggum tells us, "deep in the jungle primeval by the inmates of a Guatemalan insane asylum." Homer goes on an immersive hallucinogenic trip, complete with Johnny Cash as the voice of a talking coyote, which launches him on a journey to find his soul mate.

I've had as many hot sauce overdoses as any garden-variety chilihead, but I've never had a full-on psychedelic experience induced by chilies. One hot sauce overdose in particular, however, did reveal to me the power of the flood of brain chemicals triggered by a heavy dose of capsaicin.

At the NYC Hot Sauce Expo in 2015, I took a chili challenge at the Voodoo Chile booth. In order to hop on what Voodoo Chile's president and "Chief Sauceologist" Thomas Toth calls the "Endorphin Express," I had to tangle with his scorpion pepper tincture, which weighs in at a daunting 3,278,000 SHU. For comparison, that's roughly eighteen times hotter than Dave's Insanity Sauce, 650 times hotter than Tabasco, 1,300 times hotter than Huy Fong Foods' Sriracha, and about twice as hot as the hottest chili pepper known to humankind, a cultivar of *Capsicum chinense* known to the world as the Carolina reaper. It was not a pleasant experience—at first.

I was made to eat one small dollop and stand with Toth at his booth without spitting or ingesting anything else—so, no milk, no beer, not even water. After two minutes, I had a thirty-second window in which to bail or to go all in and eat another dollop for another two-minute stretch.

Under those conditions there is no effective cooling method available except for the devil's bargain of forming your mouth into the whistling shape and inhaling sharply; a devil's bargain because the breath somehow seems to burn even worse on its way out. One has only to stand and be with the pain. The key is to remind yourself that the whole thing is a trick of the mind. Toth's scorpion pepper tincture burned worse than anything I tasted before or since, like 3.278 million tiny ember-hot knives dancing around my mouth, but relief of a metaphysical sort came by simply reminding myself that the hot knives were an illusion.* There was no real damage being done. Practitioners of mindfulness-based stress reduction use meditation techniques to achieve a similar effect to help people suffering from chronic pain. The idea is to help them identify and isolate their pain and ultimately decouple it from other sources of suffering that physical pain can evoke, like fear and hopelessness.

There's a Zen-like pleasure in this part of the experience, in which the overwhelming pain takes hold of your complete attention and reins in your focus to the immediate experience of *now*, allowing a sense of presence and a kind of meditative peace to arise within. Studies of people who participate in sexual sadomasochism have found a similar effect, in which those receiving pain report an improvement in what researchers call "flow," the pleasurable sense of

---

* One wonders if it is entirely coincidental that the most extensive evidence of the use by prehistoric humans of hallucinogenic mushrooms comes from the chili pepper heartland of Mexico.

total focus one has when fully immersed in a task. Studies of masochists have also shown that the experience of intense pain can lead to temporarily diminished brain function in the dorsolateral prefrontal cortex, a part of the brain associated with distinguishing the self from "other"—intense pain may thereby trigger that sense of oneness your yoga instructor is always prattling on about.

Once the allotted time had passed, I chugged a beer and speed-walked toward the bathroom, doubling over for a moment as the stuff hit my stomach and my gut flinched into a smoldering knot. When I reached the sink, I opened a faucet of cold water and put my mouth under it for two minutes or so. (As an emergency measure, simply putting something cold in your mouth can cool down the relevant pain receptors so that the capsaicin effect is temporarily inactivated.) Then I made a beeline for the ice cream stand, cut to the front of the hot sauce ice cream line making hand signals to indicate my predicament to a sympathetic crowd—this was a hot sauce festival after all—and sucked down an entire pint of Bonfatto's Spice Cream's Whodathunkit?! Sweet Peachy Heat Wave. For hours after the pain subsided, I felt simply marvelous, like a creature made of clouds and light—clear, pleasant, calm, and energetic, but not anxious. This was my brain under the influence. I was high as a kite on hot sauce.

The lighthearted and wobbly high we get when we first fall in love is chemically unsustainable. In time the brain weans itself off its norepinephrine and dopamine habit by replacing those two lust drugs with a neurochemical called endorphins, the True Love drug. Endorphins act as the body's natural painkiller by binding to opiate receptors to block the transference of pain signals. Endorphins also reduce stress, lower anxiety, enhance the immune system, and give us feelings of euphoria, comfort, and attachment. Medicinal painkillers like morphine and codeine work similarly to endorphins, but they aren't broken down as readily by the body's natural processes.

By binding to opiate receptors for significantly longer than good old-fashioned endorphins, narcotic opiates increase and extend the feeling of euphoria and lead to long-term dependence.

After initially being overstimulated by the capsaicin in hot sauce, substance P levels in the body drop, which in turn reduces the body's sensitivity to pain, hence the common use of capsaicin in topical anesthetics. The substance P domino effect also causes the brain to release a flood of endorphins, which explains another part of the painkiller effect of chili peppers that so many cultures have enjoyed over the centuries.

For Karl and Helen, that rush of endorphins from both being near one another and from the chili peppers in their food was a one-two punch that reinforced their intimacy, as they literally got high on chilies and each other. When Karl and Helen were in the kitchen chopping chilies for spicy meals for their friends, dousing the odd bite in Dave's Insanity Sauce, their hands and noses tingling with capsaicin, their brains under orders from all sides to release a flood of dopamine and endorphins, you might say that love was quite literally in the air.

All that helps explain the success of Graham Connolly and his wife Lindsay Otto's new hot sauce, LBI Love Potion.

Graham and Lindsay met in the early 2000s. Both New Jersey natives, they were living at the time in Alphabet City in downtown Manhattan. When he wasn't cruising around in his 1968 Mustang convertible, Graham regularly walked the neighborhood with his black pit bull and black-and-white French bulldog. He'd often pass Lindsay on the street.

"Eventually one day I just asked her out," he said. But there was one complicating factor. "She was very young," he said. Graham was in his midthirties, and Lindsay was thirteen years his junior.

She said yes and they went out for sushi and saki in fall 2006. She came back to his apartment. "Played with the dogs for a while," Graham told me. "Then she had to go meet her brother."

The next day Graham saw Lindsay online on AOL Instant Messenger. He told her he had had a great time. She did too, she said, but the age difference—it was a little much. He understood, he said. And that was that.

Fast-forward to Valentine's Day 2007. Graham was online and saw Lindsay's screen name pop up. She messaged him.

"Hey, what are you doing?"

"Um. I'm watching the Westminster dog show," he said. ". . . you want to come over?"

Six years later they were married.

Growing up in New Jersey with Italian grandparents, for Graham food was a central part of family life. But after a run-in with a hot green chili he found sitting on a windowsill when he was a toddler—he mistook it for the bell peppers he'd always liked—spicy food was not a huge part of his eating life until a visit in the early 1980s to New York City when he was twelve. The family had visited a museum uptown and went to lunch at the Saloon Bar & Grill, a popular place across from Lincoln Center on the East Side and one of the first restaurants in the city to serve buffalo wings, spicy chicken wings popularized in Buffalo, New York, in the mid-1960s. Graham was hooked.

"I always wanted another order," he told me.

As a teenager he started trying to make his own buffalo wings but found the store-bought sauce unacceptable. So he started making his own, then trying other sauces and combinations. We all know where that road leads.

When they moved in together, Lindsay came face-to-face with a small but persistent annoyance that will be familiar to hot sauce lovers and the people who love them.

"She's always like, 'Jesus Christ, you got a lot of bottles of hot sauce in the fridge,'" Graham said. In those days his tolerance for capsaicinoids wasn't superhigh, so many of his sauces didn't get eaten very often.

"She'd be like, 'You gotta clean those bottles out,' and I'm like, 'Yeah, I know.' But I never did, because, you know, the sauce doesn't really go bad."

Eventually Lindsay made peace with Graham's love for hot sauce. The couple loved to spend time on Long Beach Island, a barrier island and beach community about 10 miles and a world away from Atlantic City, and they planned to get married there. Thus, when Lindsay suggested they give their wedding guests bottles of home-made hot sauce as party favors, partly in homage to Graham's hot sauce habit, the name for the sauce seemed obvious: LBI Love Potion.

"To the beautiful island of Long Beach for its 18 miles of sandy shores, which have inspired many a love story." So reads the dedication on every bottle. A habanero-based concoction, LBI Love Potion is a medium-heat sauce with an even consistency. In addition to the aged habanero, vinegar, and salt that make up its constituent parts, the sauce incorporates a vegetable blend of onion, garlic, and carrot, which gives it both a semisweet finish and an orange glow. I fell for the sauce instantly, as did many others before me.

"And then after the wedding was over, it was so amazing, and everybody loved the hot sauce, and people were just grabbing mul-tiple bottles of it," Graham said. "Then we found out after the fact, they were like, 'I'm sorry I took like more than one bottle,' and we were like, 'Oh no, man, everybody could have taken five,' you know? It was a hit, basically." Making it official was the obvious next step, and the rest is history.

Today the sauce is available online, at Lupa, a small Italian place in Greenwich Village; at a handful of restaurants; and at retail outlets on Long Beach Island itself, and at a growing number of hot sauce shops. At least two couples have ordered cases to use as their own wedding party favors. Graham's friend's sister gave LBI Love Potion away at a birthday/Valentine's Day party.

There's good reason hot sauce looms so large in the stories of so many of our romantic entanglements. While endorphins bond us together for the long-term, the unique, evolved ability of animals to remember pain—since unless we remember it, pain serves no evolutionary purpose—ensures that hot sauce leaves a mark on our psyches. And taste too creates strong recollections; think back to your distant childhood, and I'm betting events involving tastes, be they delicious or revolting, stand out. Smell in particular leaves an especially deep imprint in our memories. Perhaps the most prominently felt of our five senses when we're cooking, smell is the only sense that connects straight to the limbic system, one of the most ancient and primitive parts of the brain, the wildling in us all that lords over our emotions. Smell, and hot sauce with it, goes straight to the heart.

In his *Swann's Way*, Marcel Proust says it best: "But, when nothing subsists of an old past, after the death of people, after the destruction of things alone, frailer but more enduring, more immaterial, more persistent, more faithful, smell and taste still remain for a long time, like souls, remembering, waiting, hoping, upon the ruins of all the rest, bearing without giving way, on their almost impalpable droplet, the immense edifice of memory."

About a decade after she and Karl moved to the United States, Helen was diagnosed with breast cancer. Conventional medicine proved ineffective, so she began traveling to Mexico for alternative treatments. In the meantime she started a side project to digitize the lists she'd made as a young girl listening to DJ John Peel on the BBC and noting the artist and title for every song he played on the radio. Today that project exists on Facebook as the John Peel Papers, unfinished. After five years battling the disease, Helen died of cancer.

"Because I'm not with my wife, cooking's kind of been difficult," Karl told me. "I've been cooking for myself, but that's the weird thing when someone passes in your life. It took me ages, but I'm still cooking some of the stuff we would do. I'm cooking stuff with brown rice. Trying to do Thai food. Serranos. Jalapeños. You know, it's like, when I'm chopping those, I'm thinking of her. That's a romantic thing you've got there. It's gotten easier. But it's just—I'm just kind of gliding at the moment."

3

BECOMING A HOT SAUCE NATION

"Pain is the fuel of passion—it energizes us with an intensity to change that we don't normally possess."
—Rick Warren, pastor and hot sauce aficionado, in *The Purpose Driven Life*

It's one of the great quirks of culinary history that chilies spread fast around the world but took their time making their way much farther north than central Mexico. There is no archaeological proof of the presence of chilies in southern Texas, Arizona, or New Mexico in antiquity, and for hard evidence of their introduction into what is now the United States we have to credit a rather unsavory character.

The conquistador Juan de Oñate may have introduced the chili plant to what is now the southwestern United States when he was sent to investigate the northern expanse of New Spain in 1598. A war criminal by any modern standard—after meeting resistance from the Acoma people he massacred and enslaved hundreds of civilians, including children, and ordered the left foot of every man over the

35

age of twenty-five amputated*—Oñate wins no awards for the way he went about introducing Europeans to the territory we now call New Mexico, but he may have given the state the chili pepper that its residents love so dearly today. The chili he brought to his outpost in Santa Fe was likely a variety later known as the Colorado, an unreliable and disease-prone strain that nonetheless provided the raw material New Mexico farmers and later scientists hybridized and selected to, over time, develop the Hatch chili cultivar, which forms the backbone of New Mexican cuisine. A pyrrhic victory for New Mexican chiliheads, perhaps, but a victory nonetheless.

But absence of evidence is not evidence of absence. We know that robust north-south trade networks existed between native peoples on the continent well before any European went around enslaving and conquering in the hemisphere. Once they've been dried, peppers keep quite well; therefore it's plausible that those routes would have brought the chili to at least the southern reaches of the land north of the Rio Grande.

With more than a thousand years of documented history as a place of residence for humans, the Taos pueblo abutting the Sangre de Cristo mountain range north of Taos, New Mexico, is the oldest continuously inhabited community in the United States. The Red Willow people who live there are a Puebloan tribe that speaks a dialect of Tiwa, a language that is unwritten and will remain so, the tribe says, to safeguard its integrity from the influence of outsiders and to protect the secrets of their religious rituals. A mountain stream used for drinking water passes through the middle of town. Outside stacks of multilevel adobe homes, children's bicycles lean against sets

---

* Oñate was a war criminal even by the standards of his own day. He was tried and convicted by Spanish authorities for his crimes against the indigenous peoples of New Mexico, fined, and exiled from the territory.

of traditional *hornos*, a word borrowed from Spanish that refers to the dome-shaped outdoor adobe ovens the people use to bake bread. Men run power tools to shape structural wooden beams for ancient adobe houses in various states of repair. The pueblo is an extraordinary place, a living artifact where people live twenty-first century lives in a pseudo-tenth-century setting.

Off the side of the road that runs from Taos into the hills that host the Pueblo is a small restaurant called Tiwa Kitchen, which has served Puebloan dishes inspired by traditional recipes for more than twenty years. Debbie and Ben Sandoval are wife and husband co-owners/chefs and both members of the tribe; in 2016 Ben was elected governor of the Taos pueblo. The couple grows the blue corn used in their food and sources the bison meat from the tribe's herd, which you can sometimes see from the restaurant's back porch roaming in a large enclosure that backs up to the property. Recipes on the menu were handed down primarily from Ben's grandmother.

After a failed initial attempt at showing up for breakfast (Ben and Debbie do not adhere strictly to their advertised hours of operation), I enjoyed a fabulous lunch of blue corn bison enchiladas topped with red and green chili, chokecherry tea, and a side of fry bread with, per the menu, "a steaming bowl of everyone's favorite pork red chili stew," one of the most peculiar foods that has ever passed my lips. The stew is extremely simple: boiled pork in a broth of water and red chili with undetectable amounts of salt and garlic. Three flavors alone stand out—water, pork, and red chili. The pork is an Old World addition, but I'm confident there are very few foods still in existence, with a flavor so anachronistically austere, that come as close to matching what was eaten by native peoples of the Americas in pre-Columbian antiquity.

I asked Debbie if chili had always been a part of her people's traditional food. She paused for a moment. "I think that is actually something we traded for way back," she said. "I think we got it from down south. The southern tribes grew the chili more because our growing season here is very short."

What's clear is that chili is central to their traditions to a degree reminiscent of other traditions we've already encountered in the chili pepper's Mexican heartland farther south.

"For every occasion we make chili," Debbie said. "If our kids are getting baptized, if our kids are dancing for the first time or something at the pueblo, we make a feast for them on the feast day. That includes the red chili, the horno bread, the pies, cookies, the traditional theme for every feast day. Weddings. You name it, we make chili."

Despite the lack of hard evidence for the presence of chilies in the area before they were brought there by the Spanish, I'm tempted to side with Debbie. After getting stuffed with bison enchiladas and an ancient-tasting red chili stew, my gut tells me the Red Willow people have been familiar with chilies for a very, very long time.

For the most part, though, chilies were simply not present in Native American cuisine of what is now the United States before the arrival of Europeans. The lack of unassisted natural distribution very far north makes some sense, since they are, essentially, a warm weather crop. (Growers report that chilies sometimes even tend to be spicier in hotter years.) Some experts believe with good reason that the antimicrobial properties of chilies made them especially attractive to preindustrial societies in hotter, wetter, more fungal-prone climates, a need that became less urgent the farther north one traveled. Others surmise that chilies may be more popular in hotter climates because they can induce sweating without physical exertion, acting as a kind of natural, gastronomical air conditioner.

Rather than via natural animal distribution or ancient trade routes, chilies appear to have come to most of the early United States primarily through the two nonnative peoples who were the first to settle on North America's Eastern Seaboard: Europeans (primarily the English) and—as with so many of the best and, in a word, spiciest ingredients in American culture—enslaved Africans.

The eighteenth-century English botanist Phillip Miller writes in his *Gardener's Dictionary** of finding gastro-medicinal uses for chilies, including that they are an excellent way "to break and diffuse the wind, both in the stomach and the guts." (Sound familiar?) For good measure, he also gives us a description of what looks to be an early evolutionary stage frat boy: a fellow eighteenth-century Englishman who would mix chili powder "with the snuff to give others diversion but it causes violent fits of sneezing as to break the blood vessels of the head, as I have observed of some to whom it has been given." During the American Revolution, a British officer captured at Fort Ticonderoga writes of the freezing winter of 1778–79 that, without access to any stiff drink, the dispirited officers, "to comfort themselves, put red pepper into water, to drink by way of a cordial." George Washington was known to grow peppers in his gardens, as was Thomas Jefferson, who wrote, "Of the pepper I know little except that it grows in very great abundance in the prairies west of the Sabine [River, in southern Texas and Louisiana] & that it is with the Spaniards & Savages, an article in as great use as common Salt is among the inhabitants of the U.S."

Remember that Africans, by way of the Portuguese, were some of the first people on earth to come into possession of the chili pepper.

---

* For fans other than myself of that era's titles, the full thing is *The Gardener's Dictionary Containing the Method of Cultivation and Improving the Kitchen, Fruit and Flower Garden, also, the Physik Garden, Wilderness, Conservatory, and Vineyard, Interspers'd with the History of Plants, the Characters of Each Genus, and the Names of All the Particular Species in Latin and English, and an Explanation of All the Terms Used in Botany and Gardening.*

Varieties of the plant may have first made it to America by way of the transatlantic slave trade.

In 1748, the Swedish naturalist Peter Kalm visited Philadelphia on a trip through colonial America. His account of that visit includes mention of black people in the city growing okra and of gardens planted with *Capsicum annuum*, which, he said, was used in a wide variety of recipes. "Or," Kalm wrote, "the pods are pounded whilst they are yet tender, and being mixed with salt are preserved in a bottle; and this spice is strewed over roasted or boiled meat, or fried fish, and gives them a very fine taste." This is the earliest description I have seen of a bottled condiment made of chili peppers—the foundation of America's hot sauce tradition.

The Datil pepper, a hot but fruity variety much loved and celebrated today in the beautiful old coastal town of St. Augustine, Florida—one of the oldest European settlements in the Western Hemisphere—bears a close resemblance to an African pepper, the Fatalii, and may have been introduced as a result of the vile institution of slavery. On the other hand, according to local lore and the side of many a Datil pepper hot sauce bottle, indentured laborers from the Mediterranean island of Minorca brought the peppers to town. Historian David Nolan has found evidence in an old newspaper account that the Datil was introduced by a jelly maker in the 1880s, who ordered the seeds from Cuba.

In any case, the sweet and spicy Datil has a firmly rooted place in St. Augustine's culture, and today at any of the several hot sauce shops in town you can find Datil pepper hot sauce with names like Dat'l Do It and Dat's Nice. If you look hard enough you might find my personal favorite, Chef Phil's Mango Datil Sauce, a thick, meaty concoction of Datils, mangoes, apples, and oranges created by chef Phil Brown, who teaches at a culinary school in town. The Datil is about ten times hotter than a jalapeño, "but it's much more of a fruity type of heat," Chef Phil told me. "It lends itself very well in many different applications. I put it in my BBQ sauce and hot sauce but also Datil pepper sausage. So many applications." Making his sauce is highly labor intensive, and it isn't in regular production yet, though Phil says someday it might be. For now it can sometimes be found at a local farmer's market or at Hot Stuff Mon, for eighteen years running the oldest hot sauce shop in town.

Chef Phil first made his Mango Datil Sauce for Chanel St. Clair, who owns the shop Hot Stuff Mon with her husband, Bob. You're likely on any given day to find Chanel in the shop grooving to Chuck Berry–era rock 'n' roll. "My music, some people don't like it," she told me when I stopped by one sunny spring day. "I got a friend who's always trying to put on country music. I say, nah. They like it. People who come in here, they kiss, they hug. The crowd that comes in here, it's like rock 'n' roll sometimes." Chanel and I got to talking about our shared favorite brand of pickles. She was out of stock in the store but refused to let me out the door without three spears in a ziplock bag from her personal stash to go with my haul of Datil pepper sauces.

Enslaved Africans almost certainly deserve credit for the existence of the fish pepper, a peculiar heirloom breed from the Chesapeake Bay area that is today threatened with extinction. One of the most unusual looking chilies in cultivation, the fish pepper has green-and-white foliage with pods that range in different stages of development from solid green to orange to a near-black purple to fire-engine red. At times fish peppers will have their most striking feature, a rainbow of dramatic stripes running the length of the pods.

The first mention in print of this conspicuous chili comes to us from a Philadelphia recipe book in 1901. But in their *Chasing Chiles: Hot Spots Along the Pepper Trail*, which traces the history and future prospects for chilies in a world facing catastrophic climate change, authors Kurt Michael Friese et al. hypothesize that the fish pepper didn't warrant an earlier mention in print simply because white colonists in the Americas thought it suitable only as an ornamental plant. Americans of African extraction in the region, however, are known to have made frequent use of the fish pepper in spicy sauces for terrapin, oysters, crabs, and other seafood harvested from the once-bountiful Chesapeake Bay from the area around Washington, DC, north to Philadelphia. The largely oral traditions in those communities would not have prioritized documenting fish pepper uses in text, but culinary historian Michael Twitty traces the linguistic ancestry of one of those fish pepper concoctions, a relish known as piccalilli, to a Caribbean sauce, *pilipili*, a word in several sub-Saharan languages for both chili peppers and hot sauce, which in turn is linked to the words *berbere*, *fulful*, and *filfil*, which, like the word *pepper* itself, were once used in North Africa and the Middle East for black pepper and later applied to capsicums as Old Worlders tried to make sense of the bizarre New World fruit. All good evidence points to fish peppers, like most enslaved Africans, coming to the United States via the Caribbean, the primary hub for the transatlantic slave trade.

A changing American economy and ruinous environmental degradation in the twentieth century wrought wholesale destruction on the small-scale oyster shacks and seafood of Chesapeake Bay. As they vanished, those mom-and-pop establishments took much of what remained of the fish pepper sauce traditions with them. Few fish peppers are in cultivation today, and Slow Food USA includes the pepper in its Ark of Taste, a catalog of unique foods facing extinction.

Today fish pepper sauce is extremely rare, but you can intermittently find it available for retail sale under the name Snake Oil at Woodberry Kitchen in Baltimore, a rustic-hip restaurant with an aesthetic anchored by exposed brick, steel, and reclaimed wood with a grounding in locally sourced, farm-to-table fare. It opened in 2007 in a hulking old foundry called the Clipper Mill, which has been converted into condos, parking, and space for Woodberry Kitchen.

The recipe for Snake Oil is a creation of Woodberry Kitchen's chef-owner Spike Gjerde. First, fish peppers are fermented, after which vinegar and salt are added. The simple, three-ingredient concoction brings out the fish peppers' peculiar flavor—it is certainly unique.

Snake Oil wins hands down for its whimsical bottle. In keeping with the hot sauce's name, it looks like a small bottle of elixir you might have bought from a traveling huckster a century ago. Prescription-Strength Hot Sauce announces the front label (confusingly, since the sauce is relatively quite mild, but it's snake oil, so maybe that's intentional). On the back is a list of further medicinal uses, to wit: "Other claims, in addition to Excellent Digestion, include: May improve your Alertness. Will improve meat dishes & cocktails when Seasoned to Taste. Five out of 5 loyal customers believe this remedy can be SHARED to win friends and curry favor."

The culinary historian Charles Perry traces the origins of commercially produced bottled hot sauce to the seventeenth-century English and their early colonial contacts in East Asia. British food had for centuries played the role of the adoring little cousin to French cuisine, constantly imitating and never very well. But as French cooking turned away from spice-laden medieval dishes and toward the flavors of ingredients themselves, and thus especially meat-stock sauces, English gourmets complained of how expensive it was to reduce a beef coulis. Instead, the British took inspiration from the pickled fruits and vegetables—and sauces—they encountered during their colonial forays into India. London merchants were soon producing cheap imitation sauces of all sorts—mushroom soy sauce, ketchups of varying kinds, Worcestershire sauce—and bottling them for sale.

An advertisement for a bottled cayenne pepper sauce from a Massachusetts newspaper in 1807—the earliest known record of what may have been a hot sauce manufactured for commercial purposes in the United States—would have emerged from this tradition. "It all goes back to that pathetic, sad-ass, cheapjack, penny-pinching attempt of seventeenth-century Englishmen to make imitation soy sauce," says Perry. "And for that we must be grateful to them."

Over the ensuing decades many newspapers included advertisements for pepper sauces. As mainstream America in the East was slowly becoming more acquainted with the alien idea of hot pepper sauce, the country was also expanding into lands that had long nurtured a love for chilies. On October 30, 1846, newspaperman John Brown wrote a dispatch out of Santa Fe, New Mexico, for *The Anglo American*. Months earlier war had broken out between the United States and Mexico. It still raged, but the Americans had taken control of the province of New Mexico and Brown had presumably been deployed to give an accounting of this newly acquired territory. His article, "Life in New Mexico," is concerned almost exclusively with food.

"Red pepper sauce, which is simply the peppers stewed—or another dish, red peppers preserved in corn-stalk molasses—do not go badly, when you get used to them," he writes. "Albeit, before you know exactly what they are, and dip a little too deeply into the dish, they prove somewhat calorific in the region of the thorax." Don't they ever.

Charles Perry disputes that the early Massachusetts cayenne pepper sauce, and other early bottled sauces like it, were truly spicy. "Number one, Massachusetts: home of the fish cake and boiled New England dinner. It was as allergic to hot spices as old England was at that time," he says. "Another reason: they would have been making it with vinegar and so they would not have extracted much if any of the capsaicin from the chilies and they would have had basically a vinegar that had kind of the aroma of chilies. And that may have been just what they wanted."

Be that as it may, we have evidence of considerably spicy hot sauces in certain corners of the United States in the early nineteenth century. A January 11, 1845, dispatch from St. Louis, Missouri, includes a beautifully recounted—and, one suspects, a bit embellished—tale in *The New World: A Weekly Family Journal of Popular Literature, Science, Art and News* entitled "Swallowing Oysters Alive." The story tells of a visitor from the Sucker State—an old nickname for Illinois that I'm sure the Land of Lincoln would be all too happy to forget—henceforth referred to as "the Sucker."

The Sucker wandered late one evening into a St. Louis oyster house. He was tall and wore an unusual sealskin cap and ragged, ill-fitting clothes. The Sucker (depicted here as basically a redneck from the then-frontier land of Illinois) wanted to try an oyster. He asked if any were to be had.

"Yes, sir," said the server, "and fine ones they are, too."

The Sucker had neither tasted nor seen an oyster before, and after tense negotiations he agreed to trade two live chickens for a dozen oysters. "Now mind," said the Sucker, "all fair—two chickens for a dozen. You're a witness," he said, turning to a bemused local having a meal at the bar beside him. "None of your tricks," said the Sucker, "for I've hearn that your city fellers are mity slippery coons."

The Sucker rolled up his sleeves, and no sooner had his first oyster arrived than he jettisoned it down his throat. The local witness to his side dropped his fork and knife and gawked in mock amazement. "Swallowed alive as I'm a Christian," he said, feigning shock.

"What on earth's the row?" asked the Sucker.

"Did you swallow it alive?" asked the local.

"I swallowed it alive jes as he gin it to me!" cried the Sucker.

"You're a dead man!" the local said. "The creature is alive and will eat right through you."

Overcome with panic, the Sucker cried out in desperation and pleaded for help. "Don't let the infernal sea toad eat me afore your eyes!"

"Why don't you put some of this on it?" the local suggested, pointing, as the newspaper recounts the incident "to a bottle of strong pepper sauce."

"The hint was enough—the Sucker upon the instance, seized the bottle, and desperately wrenching out the cork, stalled half the contents at a draught. He fairly squealed from its effects, and gasped, and blowed, and pitched, and twisted, as if it were coursing through him with electric effect, while at the same time his eyes ran a stream of tears. At length becoming a little composed his waggish adviser approached almost bursting with suppressed laughter, and inquired— 'How are you now old fellow—did you kill it?'"

"Well, I did, hoss—ugh o-o-o-my inards. If that *Ister* critter's dying agonies didn't stir a ruption in me equal to a small earthquake then 'taint no use sayin' it—it squirmed like a serpent when that killin' stuff touched it." The Sucker said he would not pay any chickens for the experience and made a hasty exit as the others erupted in laughter.

Whatever was in that bottle, we can safely say it wasn't *not* spicy. And, though we've seen that the poorly documented early history of hot sauce in the United States offers only faint guideposts to help us track its trajectory, there's a very good reason hot sauce would have established an early foothold in St. Louis: the Gateway City straddles the Mississippi River, at the end of which, where it drains into the Gulf of Mexico, is an old city in a swamp where the story of hot sauce in America becomes richer yet, to which we will turn later.

But the question for us now requires us to hark back to Dorg and Crag. What kind of person intentionally inflicts on himself what the poor Sucker experienced? And having done so once, what kind of person does it again and again?

And, for heaven's sake, *why*?

4

VOODOO CHILE

Pain is weakness leaving the body.
—US Marine Corps (apocryphal)

Baron Ambrosia watched with some discomfort as his wife walked up in front of the others and smeared chili pepper infused hot oil over her belly and breasts. No one else knew she'd been trying for a year to get pregnant. The room in the basement of a Haitian restaurant in the Brooklyn neighborhood of East New York was thick with tobacco smoke that glowed around the flickering candlelight. They were hours into the ceremony, and the Scotch bonnet pepper-mash homemade rum that Baron brought with him was having its intended effect. The pace had become frenetic with beating drums and roaring songs in Haitian creole. It was November 2, Fete Gede, Haitian Vodou's Day of the Dead.

Initiates periodically came under the possession of various Loa, the spirits that populate Vodou's intricate cosmography. As some fell into a trance, the others would feed them from a big gourd— a mix of salted mackerel, yucca, and plantains, all drizzled in the hot chili oil. The same was offered like Communion to everyone present.

Haitian Vodou is a syncretic faith, similar to Santeria and often rendered in English as Voodoo, that combines elements of the slave traders' Catholicism with the symbolism and traditional religions of enslaved Africans. On this day—not coincidentally Catholicism's All Souls' Day—the faithful gather to commune with the Gede, a family of Loa associated with death and fertility presided over by the spirit Baron Samedi. A notoriously mischievous and profane jokester, Baron Samedi is typically depicted as a man with a skull for a face and wearing a top hat and tuxedo in black and purple. He's almost always clutching a cup of Clairin, a kind of unrefined bathtub hooch often steeped in chilies when used in rituals to contact the Loa. He's generally smoking a cigar or a pipe, and he likes black coffee and grilled peanuts. Like the Greek god Zeus, he's known to seduce mortal women, but when he's not chasing tail, Baron Samedi welcomes the dead to the underworld or helps heal those whose time has not yet come. Baron Ambrosia had brought a small black-and-purple coffin as an offering to Baron Samedi.

As Baron Ambrosia's wife returned to her seat, her belly covered in a thick, spicy oil, one of the priestesses came under the possession of Baron Samedi. Samedi began crying out in creole. Ambrosia couldn't understand, but someone else finally shouted that the spirit was saying, "Someone here has my name."

"That's *you*, Baron, that's *you!*" another of the initiates said.

Samedi looked right at Ambrosia. "You have my name," he said. "I have your name. You do me well, everyone in your house, everything in your house, will be great." The possessed moved on to someone else.

This was not Baron Ambrosia's first Vodou ceremony, but he was no less stunned by the exchange. He felt hopeful. Later, he called Rose, a Vodou priestess who had first invited him to a ritual months earlier, to thank her for including him and his wife in the Fete Gede ceremony.

"I talked to the spirits at night afterwards, after the party," Rose said. "Baron says thank you for the coffin and he has a gift for you. He sent you a gift. I don't know exactly what it means, but he sent you a gift."

A week later Baron's wife was pregnant.

I heard about Baron Ambrosia one evening while on a patio in New York City suspended several stories over Greenwich Village with my friend Natty Adams, coauthor of the book *I Am Dandy* and, appropriately, an extremely sharp dresser, along with the illustrator and writer Allen Crawford, formerly known by the awesome pseudonym Lord Breaulove Swells Whimsy. We were drinking beer and chatting about nothing: the summer suit Natty was then having designed; Allen's latest project meticulously illustrating Walt Whitman's *Song of Myself*; how weird I got at Burning Man; the ongoing bet Natty and I have about how many times we can get the phrase *leather chaps* into a book (point Nicks). Eventually talk turned to the new hot sauce project I was then still wrapping my head around.

Natty turned to Allen.

"He needs to meet Baron Ambrosia," he said.

They told me about a man who curls his hair in shotgun shells and drives around the Bronx in an ostentatious purple convertible. Always up to one scheme or another, they said.

President of the Bronx Pipe Smoking Society.

Host of an annual invitation-only dinner with dishes constructed around wild beasts like bobcat, raccoon, porcupine, and skunk.

Organizer of a recent birch wine tasting in an off-limits river cave in New York City.

Presently working on some kind of hot sauce license.

I was intrigued.

Baron is a member of a venerable old society of scientific pioneers, the Explorers Club, along with the likes of Robert Peary

(North Pole), Sir Edmund Hillary (Mount Everest), and Neil Armstrong (the moon). I arranged to meet him one afternoon at the club's headquarters off Madison Avenue in New York City's Upper East Side.

We sat across from one another on red leather chairs in a lounge off the main foyer, among glass-entombed artifacts, dramatic oil paintings of angry animals and daunting landscapes, and a fireplace flanked by two enormous ivory tusks. The place positively exudes leather-bound-bookness and—even when one is wearing Wrangler blue jeans and red Chuck Taylors, barely passed biology, and is by no plausible definition a scientist—has a way of making one feel almost respectable.

Baron wore a sharp, dark suit vest and black velveteen hat, and he brought homemade castoreum schnapps for us to sip as we talked. In case you're wondering (and I can promise you that I was), that's hooch infused with a secretion from a beaver's castor sacs, glands located near the anus and genitals, which tends to mix with discharge from the latter two organs during the secreting, and which possesses a very pungent odor indeed. It remains one of the most terrifying spirits I've ever laid to my lips, and where I come from your dad's best friend, who once pulled his own wisdom tooth in his garage with no more than a jug of whiskey and a pair of pliers, gifts you a big bottle of rotgut moonshine on or around your twenty-first birthday. The point is, if Baron Ambrosia decides to do something, he does it in style.

Long before he became Baron Ambrosia, Justin Fornal was born in the mid-1970s in Killingworth, Connecticut, an old New England town, with a population of about four thousand and so quaint as to be spooky. "Like *The Witches of Eastwick*," he told me. He grew up on a twelve-acre property in a house set back in the woods down a long dirt driveway. It was the kind of spread where a kid could explore the farthest reaches of his imagination, stomping for an eternity through birch forest, climbing trees, hunting arrowheads.

"We always ate very well," Justin said, on account of his grandparents' ethnic profile. On his mother's side, it was Italian made from scratch: homemade crab sauce linguine, pasta fazool. His father's side served Polish and Ukrainian food: homemade pierogis and golumpkis. On a night out, mom always ordered some kind of roast chicken, dad the chicken parmesan. At home, meals were made with love and by hand. What they were not was in any way spicy.

"I was always intrigued by the idea of things being spicy, but the only person I think ate anything spicy was my mother's brother," Justin said. "He's just a wild party animal. A nut. He's a nut." On his father's side, the cautionary tale of Cousin Mickey had reached the status of family lore.

"They'd always talk about how Cousin Mickey got really drunk and ate a bunch of jalapeño peppers and ended up in the hospital," he said, modulating his voice to imitate a relative. "'Ooooo! If you eat spicy food, you gonna *Cousin Mickey*!' It sounded like he had alcohol poisoning, but they were like, 'It was the peppers!' So, growing up it was like, 'Yo, if you eat spicy food, you're gonna end up in the hospital. And of course that didn't stop me at all."

Beginning with an order of buffalo hot wings in around the third grade, Justin embraced chilies and hot sauce with adolescent zeal. Chili pepper–eating challenges went hand in hand with pull-up contests and eating races—remember Dorg and Crag?—and like any serious chilihead, Justin's lust for chilies grew along with his tolerance for capsaicinoids. "So I got more and more obsessed with the heat," he said, "I just would want it all the time."

His heedless, lusty love affair with chilies peaked on a night in New York in the early 2000s. He'd gotten a degree in filmmaking at the University of Pittsburgh, followed a girl named Kim to the

Bronx, and worked in the city at a tobacco shop and as a beginning guerrilla filmmaker. Kim told him about a fabled phaal curry served at Brick Lane Curry House in the city. It was said by some to be the hottest curry on earth, clocking a reported 1,000,000 SHU. They planned to grab dinner there one evening before touring New York's recently opened Museum of Sex.

"Up until this point, everywhere I would go if we'd go out to dinner, Indian or Thai especially, they'd say, 'Oh, what spice level would you like your food?' And I said, 'I'd like it an 11. If you're saying 10, I want 11.'" By then he considered himself a professional-grade spicy food eater and had trouble getting chefs to make dishes spicy enough for him. "If I wasn't sweating and my nose wasn't running, I wasn't getting my fix."

And thus Justin took the Brick Lane Curry House phaal challenge with reckless abandon. As he ate, his cheeks and throat swelled. His stomach went into open revolt. But Kim egged him on, and he committed to finishing the dish. He would leave victorious or in an ambulance.

He finished the meal, took a sip of beer, walked outside and had a ferocious vomit in a garbage can. Today he is a member of the Phaal of Fame, as it is known. But that night he was in no mood for the sex museum, proof that in hot sauce as in the rest of life you can have too much of a good thing, even a real-deal, scientifically confirmed, bona fide aphrodisiac.

Justin is far from the first fella to be egged on into overindulging in capsaicin. The scientific literature suggests that social pressure—as with the macho pull-up contests and chili pepper challenges of his schooldays—often plays a significant role in getting people hooked on hot sauce in the first place.

Researchers have found a clear correlation between "sensation seeking"—a personality trait characteristic of people who seek out unfamiliar or intense experiences, even if it means risking life or limb, just for the thrill of it—and preference for spicy foods. Sensation seekers are more likely to use alcohol (remember Narama, patron saint of chili and mescal?), illegal drugs, and tobacco; to be nonconformists, averse to monotony, and less conventionally religious; and to volunteer for unconventional activities like hypnosis, gambling classes, and, bless their crazy hearts, unspecified scientific research. Scientists find that the sensation-seeking trait tends to be more present among men than women, though much of that effect may be due to social factors and to the effect on the brain of testosterone, a hormone present at notably higher levels in men than in women that fuels aggression, energetic ambition, libido, and, I think it's fair to assume, schoolyard pissing contests like pull-up competitions and chili pepper–eating challenges. A 2014 study from researchers at the University of Grenoble-Alpes, France, even found that men who produce more testosterone (as measured by levels of the hormone in their saliva) tend to use more hot sauce than men with lower levels of the hormone.

In addition, there's a well-established, perhaps obvious correlation between liking hot sauce and being frequently exposed to it. Part of this can be explained by the desensitizing effect that capsaicin has after repeated use—this is what we laymen call developing a high tolerance—but it's not just that the burn burns less over time. As University of Pennsylvania researcher Paul Rozin writes in a paper entitled "Getting to Like the Burn of a Chili Pepper," "There is a small desensitization effect which may modulate responses to chili pepper but cannot account for the liking for chili pepper. Note that chili likers report that they *like* the burn; it isn't that they fail to sense it."

Scientific research is by definition forever incomplete and always evolving, but in broad strokes we see the emergence of a certain personality type that tends to characterize the hot sauce fiend. Often, though by no means exclusively, we're talking about a male. He's the sort who personifies the old joke about the redneck's famous last words: "Hey y'all, watch this!" (Or my personal favorite variation: "Hold my beer.") He likes novel experiences and unfamiliar people and places. It stands to reason, then, that if he's able, he loves to travel. And Justin Fornal certainly loves to travel.

At the tobacco shop where he worked in New York, one day Justin met an employee of the Haitian consulate to the United Nations. Through him he was introduced to the Haitian community in New York, through them to Haitian Vodou, and thusly to Baron Samedi, from whom he took the inspiration for the main character of his television show *The Culinary Adventures of Baron Ambrosia*. Baron, for the spirit of mischief and raucous humor, and Ambrosia, for the food of the gods.

The show was a smart screwball comedy that melded straightforward culinary documentary with the fictitious and downright cartoonish shenanigans of Baron Ambrosia, a character who describes himself in one episode as a "preposterously endowed libertine of culinary lust."

In keeping with the show's willingness to blend fact and fiction without concern for one adulterating the other, the make-believe world of Baron Ambrosia bled thoroughly into real life. Though he's not quite the cartoon from the show, Justin Fornal is widely known today as Baron Ambrosia—that's how he was introduced to me and how I heard other members of the Explorers Club refer to him directly and in the third person while I waited in the lounge in advance of our first meeting. He really does dress like a kind of bizarro-world aristocrat, and his travels as the guerrilla filmmaker Baron Ambrosia are at least as much straightforward documentary as scripted fiction.

Accordingly, his feature-length movie, *Baron Ambrosia Is Dead*, echoes actual events. In the film, Baron Ambrosia has escaped from prison in the Bronx (that part, as far as I can tell, is not inspired by real life). With the help of the Vodou priestess Rose, he is put into a kind of zombie state and escapes the city in a purple coffin, which is sent down the Bronx River and eventually floats its way to Haiti, where they shot on location. Once he has arrived in Port-au-Prince, still in an undead, purgatory state, he brings a chili pepper offering to Baron Samedi, as is custom, at the oldest grave in the cemetery. Samedi permits Ambrosia to return to the land of the living on the condition that Ambrosia makes him dinner that evening. That leads to an in-depth, straight documentary sequence about the food of the Loa in Haiti and Haitian food in general, including one of Baron Ambrosia's all-time favorite foods, a condiment called pikliz, which is traditionally prepared with shredded cabbage, carrots, shallots, and garlic pickled in a vinegar steeped in Scotch bonnet peppers.

"Jesus, this is like everything I wish coleslaw was," Baron told me later of his first reflections upon encountering pikliz. "It was tangy, crunchy, and fucking spicy." In Haitian cuisine, the slaw part of pikliz is often added as an edible garnish to give a dish texture and piquant flavor. The spicy vinegar that remains becomes an essential hot sauce, called for in many a Haitian recipe and at every Haitian meal.

Cutting between shots of markets, dishes in various stages of preparation, and the ritual dinner being prepared for Baron Samedi at the cemetery, Ambrosia narrates the process of making the salty and spicy food that Baron Samedi demands and describes how the cooking, including flipping fish on a grill and peeling piping-hot cooked foods, must be done with bare hands.

"Like a game of hot potato with no end in sight, pain is considered part of the process," he says.

Later Baron told me about shooting the cemetery scene in Port-au-Prince, in which he races to deliver the dinner of salted mackerel and Scotch bonnet oil he has prepared for Baron Samedi in time to save his own skin.

"It started to take on a kind of mythological thing, the symbolism of the pepper, it being this kind of feminine, wonderful brew, poisonous but delicious, but invigorating, and endorphins," he said. "People around us are chanting, and it's more and more intense, and I drop it by mistake, and the pepper oil shoots into my eye and I'm completely blinded."

The cameraman demands a second take, Baron is screeching in pain, and Rose thinks he has fallen under the spirit of one of the Loa.

"She starts wiping these powders on my face, which made me kinda lightheaded, kind of high. So then I'm high and blinded." They get the shot and turn to leave.

"So when we leave the cemetery, all the energy was getting bigger and bigger and bigger and bigger. They close the gates of the cemetery and it was like *whooosh*. Everything had just closed off. It felt better. My eye wasn't hurting. Everything was clean, good to go. We went back and started drinking beer."

This is the Baron Ambrosia who cooked up the idea for a hot sauce licensing organization: the Order of the Pepper.

"My entire life I have tried to communicate to chefs and waitstaff that I want my food as hot as they can make it," Baron explains in a document that outlines the idea. "What I am presented with very rarely qualifies as extreme. Over the years I have even taken to going into kitchens to personally challenge chefs to out-spice me. This may seem a bit outrageous, but for people addicted to the endorphin-releasing sweat achieved by eating fiery foods it is necessary. However I do understand that restaurateurs do not want to harm their guests, waste food, or risk a dish being sent back for being too spicy. The answer to everyone's dilemma is the Order of the Pepper, extreme spice operator's license."

Baron's idea is that applicants would meet at an event officially sanctioned by the Order of the Pepper, at which they would be challenged to eat Magma, "the official curry of the Order of the Pepper," a 2,000,000 SHU dish that would be served in four-ounce "cauldrons." If you get through one such cauldron in one hour, you achieve the rank of Lava Lord with a red card; two in an hour earns you the status of Magma Chief and that level's black card; three in an hour makes you a Purple Abbot, the highest rank in the Order of the Pepper, with an appropriately purple card. Each card has the word *spicy* written in ten languages along the margins, and on the back this sentence: "Please serve the holder of this card the spiciest food you are able to prepare."

"The extreme spicy food community grows every year," Baron writes. "These events are a great way to bring like-minded eaters together. Anyone who loves hot sauce will finally know where they stand in the spice community echelon."

When I caught up with Baron Ambrosia again several months after we met at the Explorers Club, the Order of the Pepper was still in the works, but its launch date had been pushed back. He'd retired the television show, *The Culinary Adventures of Baron Ambrosia*, but kept the character alive, having adopted the identity wholesale. He'd been in Hungary, Tanzania, and its semiautonomous island of Zanzibar working on another show. He was also busy with a predictably eccentric mélange of side projects: a plan to swim the polluted and, for a two-mile stretch, entirely underground Jones Falls River through Baltimore; a plan to swim the circumference of Scotland's Isle of Islay, in honor of the two hundredth birthday of his favorite Scotch whisky, Laphroaig, which is distilled on the island; and organizing what he styled as the First Annual Abstract Pipe Making

World Championships. (To illustrate what such a competition would entail, I'll note that one entry is likely to be an enormous vessel that is smoked via a bowl implanted in the skull of a taxidermied coyote head in midsnarl. For example. So.)

The Order of the Pepper may have fallen to the back burner, but Baron was absolutely right that the community of people who enjoy spicy food grows every year. Indeed, though it had been growing steadily for decades, that community suddenly began to grow with a new ferocity at a nearly exponential rate in the first decade of the twenty-first century. Hot sauce sales began skyrocketing, new hot sauce festivals were launched, and this writer convinced himself and at least a few others that a book about the phenomenon was a good idea.

To understand why the hot sauce marketplace took a sudden leap skyward, we've got to dip back in time once again, to the months of tumult and uncertainty following the assassination of President John F. Kennedy, when America grappled with what it stood for as a nation and took a sizable, if belated, step toward correcting some of its past sins.

5

HARISSA EXPLAINS
IT ALL

Pleasure is an easy question. And pretty much all of us have similar answers. The more interesting question is the pain. What is the pain that you want to sustain?

That answer will actually get you somewhere. It's the question that can change your life. It's what makes me me and you you. It's what defines us and separates us and ultimately brings us together.

—Mark Manson

Shortly after nine in the morning, Tuesday, June 11, 1963, the Vietnamese Buddhist monk Thich Quang Duc sat on a cushion in the street at a busy intersection in Saigon, crossed his legs into the lotus position, and calmly set himself on fire. He burned himself alive to protest the persecution of Buddhists by the American-supported Catholic president of South Vietnam, Ngo Dinh Diem. Photographs of the incident ran in newspapers worldwide the next day, shocking consciences across the globe, among them that of President John F. Kennedy.

Hours after Thich Quang Duc's self-immolation, Alabama's seg-regationist governor George Wallace began his Tuesday morning by assuming a defiant stance in a doorway at the public university in Tuscaloosa in an attempt to prevent two black applicants from enroll-ing (or, rather, to earn points with his racist political base through the spectacle). In response, Kennedy used his executive authority to force the grandstanding governor to step aside, and that afternoon the president gave a historic radio and television address in which he called on Congress to pass a new law protecting the civil rights of all Americans, including black citizens, who had been left to fend for themselves since the end of Reconstruction under American apart-heid in the South and in segregated Northern cities. In the speech he reminded the country that it had been founded by people "of many nations and backgrounds" and insisted that America commit to a "worldwide struggle to promote and protect the rights of all who wish to be free." Later that evening the Ku Klux Klan murdered the civil rights activist Medgar Evers at his home in Jackson, Missis-sippi. And in August that summer, a quarter of a million Americans came together around the reflecting pool at the Washington Mall to hear Dr. Martin Luther King Jr. speak about his dream of a future in which Americans of all races would live together as sisters and brothers.

It was a busy time for the Kennedy administration. But at 10:00 AM that Tuesday morning in Washington, while photographs of a burning monk made their way to newsrooms around the world, a segregationist blowhard literally stood in the way of progress in Ala-bama, and the KKK plotted to kill Medgar Evers, Kennedy stopped for a moment in the colonnade at the White House adjacent the Rose Garden, which his wife had recently restored after decades of neglect, to meet with delegates from the American Committee on Italian Migration. The delegates had come to lodge a complaint with the president about the country's immigration policy. In his brief remarks to the group Kennedy called the United States' overtly racist approach to immigration "nearly intolerable." His comments during that short footnote to a busy day signaled a change soon to unfold that would utterly transform life in the United States and the way the country relates to the world.

For its first century in existence, the United States' policy on immigration had been no policy at all. By and large the states were left to establish their own immigration guidelines, resulting in a relatively freewheeling state of affairs, such that if you could make it to US shores in fairly good health, you could try your hand at making a life in America. In the late nineteenth and the early twentieth century that anarchic policy began to change as Congress enacted a series of increasingly restrictive immigration laws culminating in the Immigration Act of 1924. The act established a quota system under which the total number of immigrants from any given nationality would be restricted to 2 percent of the number of US residents of that nationality reported in the 1920 census. The intended effect of the act was to freeze America's demographic makeup as it was in 1920. Accordingly, the vast majority of immigration slots were reserved for emigrants from countries whence immigrants had come in decades past, chiefly Germany, the United Kingdom, Ireland, and other northern European countries. Immigration from eastern and southern European nations—like Italy, for instance—was severely restricted. Immigration from Africa and the Middle East became extremely difficult. East Asians were effectively barred from entry altogether.

Kennedy's disapproval of the national origins quota system in his remarks to the Italian migration committee on that Tuesday morning in 1963 can be read as part of a larger effort under way in his administration to correct some of the sins of America's racist past, having been spurred into action by decades of steadily growing activism on the part of civil rights leaders. In July that year, weeks after that meeting near the Rose Garden, Kennedy sent a group of suggested immigration reforms to Congress, including an end to national origins quotas.*

Kennedy's assassination in Dallas that November left the job of instituting his administration's reforms to Lyndon Johnson, who capitalized on reverence for the memory of the slain president and his own mastery of Capitol Hill politics to move the measures forward. The next year the United States passed the landmark Civil Rights Act of 1964. In 1965 Johnson signed the Voting Rights Act into law. Just months later he put pen to paper in a signing ceremony on Ellis Island, making the Immigration and Nationality Act of 1965 into law and eliminating the national origins quota system outright.

Ironically, during debate on the bill one of the key arguments made repeatedly by the proponents of immigration reform was how little actual impact the reforms would have. Critics had warned of an influx of immigrants from the poorest corners of the world, but Senate immigration subcommittee chairman Ted Kennedy, the late president's younger brother, would have none of it. Senator Kennedy championed the bill while reassuring his colleagues that it "will not flood our cities with immigrants. It will not upset the ethnic mix of our society." His brother Robert, then attorney general, made a prediction so unfathomably wrong that one has to wonder if he was simply lying to get the bill passed when he said that if the law were enacted, there would be about five thousand immigrants from Asia

---

* Incidentally, the day after Kennedy sent Congress his proposed immigration reforms, a group of boys in a program sponsored by the American Legion met the president at the White House, among them a sixteen-year-old from Hope, Arkansas, who would one day become president himself and preside over a period in which immigration to the United States boomed as a direct result of Kennedy reforms.

initially, "after which immigration from that source would virtually disappear."

"This bill we sign today is not a revolutionary bill," President Johnson said at the signing ceremony. "It does not affect the lives of millions. It will not restructure the shape of our daily lives." A parade of others reiterated the point before Congress. Rarely has any group of people, even American lawmakers, been so wrong.

The new US immigration regime created a blanket ceiling on immigrants from the Eastern Hemisphere without preference for any country or ethnicity, while giving special accommodations for family reunions and immigrants with desirable skills. The result was both a spike in immigration overall (many of the slots reserved for the northern European countries favored by the old policy had long gone unused) and a dramatic change in the ethnic makeup of the immigrant population—and eventually of the United States as a whole.

After a long decline, the share of immigrants in the total US population had bottomed out at 4.7 percent in 1970. Once the 1965 reforms were implemented, it increased rapidly: the country was 8 percent immigrant in 1990 and 13 percent in 2010.

Asians, who represented just 5 percent of the total immigrant population in 1960, were 18 percent of the total in 1980 and nearly 30 percent in 2013.

Less than 1 percent of the immigrant population in 1960, Africans made up 4.4 percent of immigrants in 2013—or, put another way, the African-born population of the United States roughly doubled every decade from 1970 on.

The top ten countries of origin in 1970 were Canada, Germany, Cuba, the United Kingdom, the USSR, Poland, Ireland, Austria, Italy, and Mexico. By 2010 they were the Philippines, Vietnam, China, Cuba, the Dominican Republic, El Salvador, Guatemala, India, Korea, and Mexico.

You may have noticed that so far in this section I've left an obvious void in discussing immigrations trends: America's neighbor to the south and the proverbial elephant in the immigration policy room.

Hispanic immigration to the United States is a special case for many reasons, not the least of which being that many of the country's original Hispanic "immigrants" had only to stay right where they were to emigrate, after the United States took control of great swaths of what was once northern Mexico following the Mexican-American War. For many decades thereafter the movement of both Americans and Mexicans across the US-Mexican border was both frequent and fluid, such that Mexican laborers could easily travel to the United States to work temporarily and return home secure in the knowledge that they could make it back to gringo country when they needed to make a buck. A temporary crackdown on migrant laborers during the Great Depression ended during World War II with the implementation of the Bracero program, a temporary workforce arrangement that gave official sanction to migrant laborers and made it relatively hassle free once again for Mexicans to earn dollars and return home without fear that they'd never be able to earn dollars again.

The end of the Bracero program in 1964 amounted to another crackdown on Mexican immigration by making it more difficult for migrant laborers to get back into the United States once they'd returned home. The immigration reforms of 1965 also imposed a cap for the first time ever on the number of immigrants allowed into the United States from the Western Hemisphere. The net result of those phenomena was an upsurge in Hispanic immigration both legal and illegal. Mexicans—who could once move more or less freely across the border and thus had no urgent need to settle permanently in the United States—represented about 6 percent of all immigrants in 1960 but nearly 30 percent by 2010. Latinos composed less than

5 percent of the total US population in 1970 but more than 17 percent in 2013.

It would be difficult to overstate the impact of this demographic change, and the cross-cultural linkages that have resulted from it, on mainstream American culture. In every cultural nook and cranny, from politics to sports to music and everything in between, the United States is a changed country today because of the immigrants that have landed on its shores in the past several decades. And it's not merely the effect of sheer numbers of foreign-born residents in the United States—we are all changed by their presence. Americans of all ethnicities are a different people today because of the influx of immigration from Latin America, Asia, and Africa.

The steady growth in popularity of soccer in the United States is partly the simple effect of more Americans in general being exposed to the game (and of some Americans developing, or at least playing at, a more global, cosmopolitan outlook), but there can be no Major League Soccer at the scale we know it today without Latino immigrants and their offspring. While English-language MLS broadcast viewership has lagged, MLS's Spanish programming picks up the slack. D.C. United fans in Washington, DC, of all skin tones and ethnic extractions cheer for their team at games with chants of "Vamos! Vamos United!" A thoroughly American art form, salsa is a dance with Latin American DNA that was born in New York City. Religions once alien to much of the United States have become thoroughly anchored in communities throughout middle America. In most states of the American West the second-largest religion is Buddhism, including in my home state of Oklahoma; the Tam Bao Buddhist Temple in Tulsa, my hometown, hosts a fifty-foot statue of Quan Am, the bodhisattva of compassion, the tallest statue of a Buddhist deity in the entire United States. The greatest fight movie of the 1980s, *Karate Kid* (sorry, *Rocky III* fans)—in which the Italian

American Daniel is educated in arts both martial and not by the Oki-
nawan immigrant Mr. Miyagi—could serve admirably as an allegory
for American life in the latter half of the twentieth century.

In politics, the effects of the United States' immigrant-fueled
cultural transformation resonate through each election cycle. In
2015 a Buddhist represented Hawaii in the US Senate, and the
House of Representatives hosted Buddhist, Muslim, and Hindu
legislators. With every campaign season comes another round of
hand wringing and prognosticating about how America's large and
growing Hispanic population will vote. Perhaps the most prominent symbol of the immigration transformation is the country's
first African American president. Though he's not technically a
product of the 1965 law, since he was born in the United States to
a Kenyan father and an American mother in 1961, the idea that a
second-generation, biracial American named Barack Hussein Obama
with roots in Africa and childhood memories in Indonesia could get
elected president by the same country that reelected Richard Nixon
simply does not stand up.

The impact of America's cultural transformation is so omnipresent it can be easy to forget it's there, but nowhere is it more evident
than at the dinner table, where so-called "ethnic food"—primarily Asian and Latin American but also cuisine from Africa and the
Middle East—is steadily grabbing market share from the European
cuisine typical of Julia Child's America. According to the National
Restaurant Association the third most popular kind of appetizer in
the United States in 2014 was ethnic street-food-inspired fare, like
tempura, *taquitos*, and kebabs (just behind charcuterie and the most
popular type, reported unhelpfully as "vegetarian appetizers," which
one is tempted to assume includes things like hummus, falafel, and
Japanese rice balls). In a 2015 survey by the market research firm
YouGov on what "types of meals" Americans prefer to eat, Mexican

and Chinese beat out barbecue, "meat and potatoes," seafood, and southern. Thai beat out French, "soul food," and vegetarian. According to a report from the business intelligence firm IBISWorld, overall food trends in the United States "include a decline in the popularity of French, German, and Scandinavian foods and a shift toward Mexican, Japanese, Thai, Caribbean, and Middle Eastern foods." You can see the change firsthand with a visit to any of the major mainstream grocery stores, which have been expanding their international aisles in recent years. A survey from the market research firm IRI projects that ethnic food retail sales in the United States, which totaled nearly $11 billion in 2013, will reach more than $12.5 billion by 2018.

It's true that the Chinese and Mexican food familiar to most Americans is in fact a kind of imitation cuisine with a foundation in the real thing but significantly altered for the American palate. General Tso's chicken, orange chicken, and chop suey do not exist in recognizable form in China, and it doesn't take a mental giant to surmise that something called bourbon chicken has roots far from Beijing. Fajitas are an American invention—or rather an invention of the Texan-Mexican fusion cuisine known to the world as Tex-Mex, which some Americans mistake for Mexican cuisine. But even Americanized dishes call for chilies and hot sauce more often and in substantially greater quantities than the European-American cuisine typical of pre-1965 America.

Furthermore, American dining trends overall reflect a country steadily leaning away, if little by little, from recipes doctored and diluted to fit American tastes. The National Restaurant Association reports that, as of 2014, the two most popular trends in ethnic cuisine were "ethnic fusion cuisine" and "authentic ethnic cuisine." (They're virtually tied.)

Hot sauce is also showing up in booze. Sure, the Prairie Fire shot (tequila or whiskey and hot sauce) has been around for a while, but there's been a decisive uptick in the appearance of spicy drinks in bars across America.

"I'm definitely seeing a trend with spicy and savory cocktails versus sweet," says Ann Tuennerman, founder of Tales of the Cocktail, perhaps America's most important spirits industry event—it takes place annually in New Orleans, a city that if it didn't invent the cocktail, as some claim, has certainly perfected drinking.

Another way to measure the degree to which hot sauce has taken up an esteemed position in America's pantheon of cultural touchstones is to examine that cherished American tradition: junk food. Wendy's has long offered a spicy chicken sandwich but has recently expanded its menu to offer more specific items, like a jalapeño burger and ghost pepper fries. That favorite mecca of stoners and late-night boozers, White Castle, now offers a jalapeño slider and a Sriracha slider. (Field tests I bravely conducted on myself concluded that neither of White Castle's spicy offerings seem to include anything like actual Sriracha or jalapeños, but I was cold sober at midday at the time, which may not be fair conditions for this sort of study.) The list of fast-food establishments incorporating spicy menu items is long and growing, but there is probably no better example of the fast foodification of hot sauce than the Thickburger El Diablo at Carl's Jr. and Hardee's. Marketed as the "hottest burger in fast food," the burger was literally designed by an advertising agency, first conceived as a way "to appeal to the large and growing Hispanic market in Carl's Jr.'s core Southwest market," reports the magazine *AdWeek*. That initial impetus eventually gave way to a burger intended to appeal to the large and growing chilihead market in general.

"Typically, hot products in fast food aren't really that hot," said Justin Hooper, creative director at 72andSunny, the ad agency that created the burger. "They have to cater to everyone. With this one, we really went all in on the hot, on the spice. We came up with the name 'El Diablo' because we want consumers to understand imme-diately that this is really the hottest burger in fast food."

We see the effect in spin-off packaged snacks. Just as the original potato chips with sour cream and onion dip that once formed the foundation of Super Bowl Sunday buffets eventually begat sour cream and onion potato chips, and just as a Frito corn chip pilaf piled high with chili con carne and cheese to make a Frito chili pie eventu-ally begat Frito chili cheese–flavored chips, so too did the hot sauce craze finally beget Texas Pete–flavored Herr's chips; Sriracha-flavored popcorn; Frank's RedHot–flavored sunflower seeds; and PepsiCo's Frito-Lay division's Tapatio-flavored Cheetos, Doritos, and Ruffles. You don't get to a Tapatio-flavored Dorito until hot sauce has gone mainstream.

"Once you've hit Frito-Lay you've kind of hit the big leagues," Matthew Hudak, a food markets analyst for the global business intel ligence outfit Euromonitor, told me.

The key point here is that while waves of immigration after 1965 added in absolute terms to the number of Americans with an affinity for spicy food, they also helped introduce it to the rest of the coun-try. Like others before them, the post-1965 immigrants enriched American culture in uncountable ways, one of which has been the mainstreaming of hot sauce. This is especially true for Americans under about thirty-five years old, who more than any other age group are driving the breakaway growth in the hot sauce market.

"It's very much a full millennial thing," Hudak said. "No matter the ethnic background, a lot of them were raised on a greater variety of cuisines."

For many Americans in the millennial cohort and younger, who came of age at a time when the post-1965 cultural transformations were already well under way, so-called ethnic food doesn't even register as exotic. For some of us it's just as likely to fall in the category of comfort food. A third-grade school project of mine, which my aunt found recently in one of those terrifyingly vast attic archives of childhood detritus, features a short autobiography in which I matter-of-factly declared my number one favorite food to be the one thing I ate most often: rice. (I had a Filipina babysitter.) When I'm feeling under the weather, I'd rather pass on the classic American chicken soup; what I really want is a steaming bowl of Vietnamese pho, spiced up with plenty of hot sauce and chilies. And I'm a fourth-generation Okie who grew up in Tulsa, which is a truly wonderful city but in the 1980s was not what one would call a bastion of cosmopolitanism.

Americans have always been prone to up and moving, and the country remains one of the most mobile on earth, but the millennial cohort came of age in the era of globalization, when moving meant interacting with an even more diverse assortment of cultures than before, resulting in a cosmopolitanism in American culture that has been good for hot sauce in the United States. Kai Saunders is an excellent example.

Kai was born in California and lived there for a grand total of about a week and a half. At four days old her parents propped her up against a couch to take her first passport photo and roughly a week later loaded her onto an airplane en route to Jeddah, Saudi Arabia, where her father was based as a commercial airline pilot for Saudi Arabian Airlines. There she spent the bulk of her childhood.

With an Indian mother and homemaker, Kai grew up eating spicy curries at home, but her English father is responsible for her earliest memory of chilies. A former pilot for the Royal Air Force and an avid traveler, Kai's father had a distinctly cosmopolitan outlook on life. "He was more into every other culture than he was England," Kai told me. Owing to policy changes after the war that opened the gates, so to speak, to colonial subjects, in the latter half of the twentieth century the United Kingdom saw a wave of immigration similar in broad strokes to what the United States experienced. His roots were firmly British, but either through his extensive travels or the influence on British culture of post–World War II immigration from the empire beginning in 1950s, Kai's father developed a fierce and unshakeable love for capsaicin. One shopkeeper at a market in Jeddah would save a tray of raw chilies just for him on days when the family would visit.

"He would just snack on them while walking around," Kai said. "I remember once just sort of being like, 'OK, I'm ballsy enough to try this now.' And I don't know, I just wanted to be cool like my dad. I just started eating these raw chilies with him while we were walking around the store getting the rest of the groceries." A chili pepper trial by fire like that can go one of two ways. The pain is a given, but the outcome of the experience hinges on how a person responds to it—and for Kai it was the beginning of a lifelong love affair.

As an American by birth, with an Indian mother and a British father and raised in Jeddah's multicultural expat community, Kai's formative years were about as international as it gets. Her best friends were Austrian. In addition to England and the United States, as a small child she traveled to Canada, Spain, France, Germany, India, Egypt, Qatar, Bahrain, and the United Arab Emirates. This was no life for a picky eater, and Kai embraced unfamiliar and spicy foods. One favorite was *harissa*, a Tunisian hot sauce (technically a chili paste) common throughout North Africa but also available in Jeddah, where she'd spread it on falafel sandwiches and shawarma.

Incidentally, though not a hot sauce Kai Saunders grew up with, the Louisiana-based hot sauce Crystal is wildly popular in Saudi Arabia. The kingdom is one of Crystal's biggest foreign markets. And, according to the blog *Stuff Saudi People Like* (I cannot vouch for its authenticity, but its posts seem legitimate in a very funny and very un-self-aware way), "Many Saudis like to carry Crystal hot sauce in their pockets." So there's that.

"Go to any dinner party in Saudi," the blog author writes, "and I am 100% positive that you will find Crystal bottles standing with pride on the dining table or on the floor (for people who like to eat on the floor)." Except, apparently, for a dinner party at Kai's childhood home.

No, for her first enduring romance with an American hot sauce Kai had to wait until her family moved from Saudi Arabia to the Saudi Arabia of America (at least as oil is concerned): Texas.

When Kai was nine years old, her father retired from the airline and the family moved to Italy, Texas, a minuscule town of fewer than two thousand people—"One of those places where the water tower is the biggest building," as Kai described it—just south of Dallas–Fort Worth. Soon thereafter they moved to Waxahachie, a bigger small town, slightly closer to Dallas. In the family's first year in Texas the town newspaper ran an article in which a reporter asked students in the elementary school what they wanted mom to make for Christmas breakfast. Kai, the new kid in school, said she hoped her mom would make masala dosa, a south Indian staple similar to a crepe, with a side of *sambar*, a spicy dipping broth. She had singled herself out as different.

"I got embarrassed about it," she told me. "I mean, when I moved to the States, I wanted to fit in, and in a country town in Texas, spicy food was not a thing. I mean, Mexican food, yes, but other ethnic food was never available."

Marked as weird by her classmates, Kai was determined to become normal. She soon started asking her mother to pack more typical American lunches. She developed a taste for french fries and peanut butter and jelly sandwiches. She broke herself of the lilting

Indian English accent she'd grown up with and even adopted an affected Texas twang. And she fell head over heels for an all-American hot sauce called Texas Champagne, a relatively mild artisanal sauce produced by Jardine Foods out of its ranch near Buda, a town south of Austin in the Texas Hill Country.

After high school Kai went off to school in Georgia, to the Savannah College of Art and Design. As food was concerned, Kai's college years in Savannah were mostly spent at a couple of Mexican joints. Sadly, she left town on the cusp of the major culinary hot sauce explosion that occurred in the first few years of the new millennium, right around the time a young married couple was opening what would become, virtually overnight, one of America's greatest hot sauce treasures: Angel's BBQ.

I heard about Angel's while traveling north along the Atlantic coast from St. Augustine, Florida, to New York City with Aric S. Queen, a travel writer and frequent travel companion doubling in this particular instance as my photographer. The route took us through Savannah, a town described in the film *Midnight in the Garden of Good and Evil* as "*Gone with the Wind* on mescaline," leaving me little choice but to stop for a night. Or two, as happens in Savannah.

Aric had been to town previously and played tour guide as we strolled past its stately antebellum houses and through its pretty squares draped in Spanish moss, easing into the slow rhythm of Savannah's unblushing beauty. After dark, Aric insisted we stop in at one of his all-time favorite pubs, Pinkie Master's, a small dive centered around a jukebox and a horseshoe-shaped bar with a well-earned reputation as a bug light for the extraordinary weirdness that lurks beneath Savannah's civilized veneer.

There's another line in *Midnight in the Garden of Good and Evil* worth mentioning here: "Rule number one: Always stick around for one more drink. That's when things happen. That's when you find out everything you want to know." This isn't good advice for every city, and in some less genteel corners of the world the danger of overstaying one's welcome makes it downright perilous. But it's sage wisdom indeed in a town as in love with its own hospitality as is Savannah.

A group of bar patrons had taken a cigarette break outside, and we stood in a huddle near the door, lighting up and making small talk. The natives asked where Aric and I were from, and I explained that we were both raised in Oklahoma. Conversation turned to the question of whether or not Oklahoma is, in a cultural sense, in "The South." (It is and it isn't—mostly it's just confused.)

"How do you like your eggs?" asked Aaron, a motorcycle mechanic from South Carolina with a nearly cartoonish southern accent, buzz-cut hair, and a close-cropped goatee. He'd walked over from the street to join our conversation and had a shop cloth around one finger held in place with a zip tie, a rudimentary bandage from an earlier mishap with a tool.

"Runny," said Aric.

"Fuckin' Yankee," Aaron said. He declined to clarify the point.

Later Aaron told a story about speeding far above the limit through the streets of Oakland, California, "ankle deep in beer cans," whereupon he passed a police cruiser and slammed on the brakes. As smoke wafted over the car, Aaron said, "I saw my life, family, and hobbies flash before my eyes!" He also spoke of a friend whose name he did not know, so, Aaron said, "I call him Memphis, 'cause, you know, he's an asshole."

He is an enigma, but sometimes you meet a person whose judgment you know instinctively to trust.

Later in the evening, after we'd stayed for more than one more drink, I mentioned that I was working on a book about hot sauce.

Aaron said I needed to go to Angel's. All present agreed. They're known for their sauces, they said, and great barbecue. I was locked in for lunch the next day.

I ate a late breakfast of vanilla ice cream, one scoop, and walked toward West Oglethorpe Lane, a tiny stretch of street in Savannah's Historic District that resembles an alley more than a service road. The street hosts the entrances to a few small parking lots, several dumpsters, the ass ends of a group of buildings, and one small carriage house painted white with barn doors. When the food is ready, a flag is displayed on one of the doors with the unambiguous shorthand: BBQ. Unless you arrive early, you can usually tell Angel's by the line stretching out from the entrance, which will generally be there until closing time (i.e., whenever the food runs out).

After he graduated from the California Culinary Academy in San Francisco, Chef Andrew Trice III spent more than a decade working in fine-dining kitchens in the Bay Area before he and wife Eileen moved to Savannah to open Angel's BBQ in 2006. The couple wanted a place small enough to run entirely by themselves, and they got it—the tiny inside of Angel's has space for just a few spots at a table, and the entire menu, from the beef brisket and pulled pork butt to the tangy mustard coleslaw and peanut collard greens, is made with refreshing homespun care. The menu is filled out by a dizzying and ever-changing array of marvelous house-made (mostly hot) sauces. I myself dressed my lunch of pork butt, baked beans, and slaw with intermittent shots of Angel Drops, Angel's House Sauce, Zog-Zog Sauce, and something with a particularly muscular kick called Beware the Jabberwock.

It's enough that Angel's slings lip-smacking barbecue and sauces prepared with heaps of TLC, but Chef Andrew's attitude about the whole enterprise inspires damn near jubilation for the writer attempting to put something on paper about America's hot sauces. It's an irritating if understandable fact of life in the world of hot sauce that, virtually without exception, hot sauce makers will not discuss their recipes in any detail. Chef Andrew, on the other hand, is beyond enthusiastic about telling the world how to make his sauces. (I'm sure it helps that he comes up with new ones all the time.) Here's Andrew neatly summarizing his outlook on the matter to a newspaper in 2014:

"Barbecue has a bit of mystique and secrecy around it, and I just want to help show people that cooking and Barbecue isn't nearly as intimidating as it may seem. People may be afraid to cook, or don't know how, and I just want to help show how simple it can be."

So committed is Trice to sharing the delights of his hot sauce that he's assembling a book of recipes, and a peculiar book it is indeed.

Titled "A Pirate's Progress" and, in homemade-galley form at least, featuring a Jolly Roger burned into the wooden cover, the volume collects some of the tastiest sauce recipes Chef Trice has concocted. It's a strange document. Here's the opening of the introduction:

"The following pages are a reproduction of a folio I discovered quite by accident three years ago in Savannah, Georgia, hidden inside the false bottom of an old sea chest. Appearing to date from the 18th century, the chest was given to me in lieu of a debt and while even a fool wouldn't deem the outside anything close to museum-quality, the inside was magic."

Inside the old sea chest was a spice box typical of the Indian subcontinent, so goes the narrative, in a chest redolent with tobacco and exotic spices, "pungent with adventure and the roiling sea." Out fell the floor of that box and out with it came . . .

"The codex was written by hand, extremely worn and sadly damaged in many places. It wasn't a logbook or a purser's ledger, but rather a collection of recipes—recipes that even the most inexperi-

A chili cultivated in the mid-Atlantic region primarily by African Americans, the fish pepper's distinctive multicolored stripes make it one of the most visually striking chilies. *Jackie Jasper, Mountainlily Farms*

Born in the Mexican town of Pochutla and a resident of Oaxaca for forty years, Esther Leonor Alonso García is the owner and chef at El Escapulario, where she makes fabulous mole, an early evolutionary ancestor of hot sauce.

A *tlayuda*—also known as a Mexican pizza—at El Escapulario is served with a hot sauce on the side of pasilla chilies, tomato, garlic, onion, and *chapulines* (grasshoppers).

Thomas Toth (right) and the author (left) after a double dose of Voodoo Chile's 3.278 million SHU scorpion pepper tincture at the NYC Hot Sauce Expo.

Baron Ambrosia at the Explorers Club in Manhattan's Upper East Side.

There is only one original Ninfa's and this is it, and they don't want you to forget it.

Annie Rupani, chocolatier, at her Houston shop Cacao & Cardamom, with her chipotle chocolate pyramid.

Chef Andrew Trice III slinging 'cue at Angel's BBQ in Savannah, Georgia, with his delightfully bizarre book "A Pirate's Progress" in the foreground.

Wilford Bouton contends with a capsaicin overdose at the Louisiana Hot Sauce Expo in Lafayette.

Anchor Bar in Buffalo, New York, where the now-famous wing sauce named for the city was invented. Sort of.

The author sinks his teeth into a bird at Gus's World Famous Hot & Spicy Fried Chicken in Memphis, Tennessee.

Solly's Hot Tamales in Vicksburg serves up some of the Mississippi Delta's best hot tamales.

The author perusing the wares at one of the many hot sauce shops that dot cities across America—this one in New Orleans.

Two Dick Billy Goat hot sauce, out of the Thunderbird Hotel in Marfa, Texas, has a flavor both delicious and unique. Two Shack investigates.

Mark Scott, the chef at the Thunderbird Hotel and creator of Two Shack's favorite hot sauce, Two Dick Billy Goat.

A small sample of hot sauces collected on a drive from New Mexico to Terlingua, Texas, a ghost town visible in the background.

enced sea cook would know by heart, things like hardtack, plum duff and lobscouse."

The codex, ostensibly written by some long-lost sot named "Rum Rat Dawson," features the full and unredacted recipes for some of Trice's most prominent preparations, like Zombie Blood (guajillo chilies, ancho chilies, chiles de árbol, plus butter, garlic, onions, honey, etc.), the Devil's Dandruff (chiles de árbol, habanero, ghost chile, paprika, etc.), and Voodoo Juice (habanero, chiles de árbol, tepin chile, ghost chile, sourwood honey, etc.). The tome is also flecked with useful advice for the seafaring foodie, like this bit of guidance on tattoo placement for luck optimization: "Cock on the right; never loosed a fight. Pig under the knee; safety at sea." Now you know.

Alas, Kai Saunders was not in town to appreciate the magnificence of Angel's. While Trice was getting the bottle rolling on his new project, Kai was moving on with life after Savannah. She got married and divorced and moved to the Washington, DC, area to raise twin boys, who as toddlers are, unsurprisingly, budding hot sauce lovers. One will eat anything, she told me, even if it's super spicy—"he'll chug water, eat bread, whatever, but he's gonna eat whatever it is"—while the other is slowly coming around.

"It's definitely something that's handed down from my parents to me, and I want my kids to have that be a part of their lives," she said, "the cultural aspect of it. I refuse to have picky kids."

Kai's kids are the culmination of seismic changes that have cleaved and smashed the cultural fabric of America, expanding the country's cultural reach beyond Europe and closer to Asia, Latin America, and Africa. The twins' English grandfather married their Indian grandmother, then moved to Saudi Arabia and Texas, where the couple raised Kai, who is now bringing up her boys in America's capital city. Their multicultural lineage would have been unlikely in the extreme half a century ago, and the same forces that brought them into being—of globalization and of liberalizing migration policies—are those that have literally spiced up American life by infusing the culture with rich and spicy cuisines.

Those changes are the direct result of concrete modifications to government policy, chiefly the Immigration and Nationality Act of 1965, which are themselves the outgrowths of a country and a world awakened by uprisings against colonialism and racism and demands that multiculturalism and diversity be celebrated—in the classroom, the courthouse, the kitchen, and beyond.

Without a Buddhist monk's fiery protest against an oppressive regime, without the steadfast work of activists and politicians to pull the United States, sometimes kicking and screaming, out of the blandness of homogeny and into the delights of diversity, without a new generation of politicians willing to push and drag the country out of bad old habits, America would not have become the hot sauce–loving country it is today. If we decided collectively to start celebrating Martin Luther King Jr. Day by going out for an especially hot sauce–drenched meal with our family and friends—well, you'd get no argument from me.

Or if not MLK Day, with hot sauce America might find a solution for the annual holiday crisis that is Columbus Day. Every year a growing chorus of Native Americans and others points out that the holiday commemorates what for the indigenous peoples of the Americas was the beginning of a centuries-long tragedy.

Christopher Columbus was, even by charitable standards, a megalomaniac who went to his grave confused about where he was, having never acknowledged he'd accidentally bumped into a continent unknown to most of Europe. And he wasn't even the first European to do that. Vikings had been to North America centuries earlier—that's right, Christopher Columbus didn't even Columbus the Americas.

Rather than celebrate Columbus, though, we might celebrate the Columbian Exchange—the unparalleled supernova of cultural intermingling that came from the meeting of two long-disconnected worlds. All Americans today are products of that exchange, and what better way to celebrate our global heritage than with hot sauce, the condiment from the Americas that traveled at lightning speed to the far reaches of the earth and back? Hot sauce is the most cosmopolitan, most multicultural of all condiments, a delicious outcome of the strife we humans have made for ourselves as we've navigated what in historical terms is the relatively new phenomenon of meeting and making friends with people very different from ourselves. If we decided collectively to celebrate Indigenous Peoples' Day by dousing dinner in hot sauce—well, you'd get no argument from me there, either.

6

COOKING
WITH CHILIES
IN H-TOWN

Like I said before, your body is not *a temple, it's an
amusement park. Enjoy the ride.*
    —Anthony Bourdain, *Kitchen Confidential*

Hot sauce is a peculiar ingredient. There's the fact that unlike
virtually all other ingredients, the key constituent of hot
sauce, capsaicin, imparts not a taste but a temperature sensation.
There is of course the fact that unlike other ingredients capsaicin
has the capacity to hurt the eater. And there's the fact that hot
sauce is a condiment, typically added as a final embellishment to a
dish rather than as an integral component of it. Cooking with capsaicin can be a delicate operation requiring a keen sense of balance,
and to learn the intricacies of the art I decided to talk to a chef
about how it's done. What better place for such an investigation
than the tip of the spear, the metropolis that typifies America's
post-1965 transformation into a hot sauce hub: Houston, Texas,
the biggest city in the South and the one America loves to hate.

A friend once nicely summed up the general attitude many have toward Houston by describing for me a hypothetical day in America's fourth-largest city: "baking to death in a steel box on a concrete highway in hours of traffic, endless suburban sprawl, crawling for your last drink into a noisy Pappadeaux surrounded by a parking lot of Infiniti SUVs and a few trashy strip clubs as the only glimmer of redemption." Well then.

Houston haters always harp on the clogged highways and McMansions, and they are not wrong. Houston has both at a scale that begins to test the limits of human imagination. But I've discovered a trick for enjoying Houston if you don't like interstate traffic and suburban sprawl: stay off the interstate and out of the suburbs.

I have a great affinity for Texas, and not just because of my natural affinity for things that register as terrible (pop country, tiny powdered donuts, moonshine, etc.). The Texas landscape is varied and expansive in a combination that makes for striking natural beauty, from the eastern pines to the near-empty wastelands of the Panhandle. And among Texans there really is a shoulders-back swagger that can be charming when it isn't compensating for deficiencies elsewhere. Taken altogether the state is fabulously diverse. And while San Antonio has its charm and history, and Austin clings fiercely to the vestiges of its once-legendary weirdness, and Dallas is over there being Dallas, nowhere is Texas's big, bad, swaggering diversity on bigger, badder, more swaggering display than in its biggest city, named for the only American to have served as both a governor and a foreign head of a state,* Sam Houston.

Diversity is a difficult thing to measure—do you delineate the area you're measuring by metro area? City limits? Census tract? City

---

* Of the Republic of Texas, in case that wasn't obvious, from 1836 to 1838 and 1841 to 1844.

block? On the whole, individual households are sure to be the most ethnically homogenous places in America. You get the picture—but by any measure Houston is one of America's most diverse cities, and according to the metrics used by researchers at Rice University's Kinder Institute, as of 2010 Houston surpassed New York City to become the most diverse big city in the country. In Houston, every racial and ethnic category is now a demographic minority. And speaking of those suburbs, the two most ethnically diverse cities in the region are the suburbs of Missouri City and Pearland, more diverse even than Houston itself.

Houston's extraordinary quilt of ethnicities and cultures owes to the fact that before the 1960s, Houston was a city of fewer than one million, relatively small compared with the populations of Los Angeles, Chicago, and New York. As Houston rocketed up the population rankings of American cities, in tandem with the rise of car culture, air conditioning, and the American oil business, it grew roughly 20 percent per decade in the post-1965 era. What happened to Houston demographically is thus a microcosm of what happened to the country as a whole, and where goes Houston tomorrow goes the United States. "Houston is 25 years ahead of the rest of the country," Kinder Institute codirector Stephen L. Klineberg told *Smithsonian* magazine. "Soon all of America will look like this city. There is no force in the world that can stop the United States becoming more Latino, more African-American, more Middle Eastern, and Asian. It's inevitable!"

The result is a garden of delights for the culinary adventurer—particularly one interested in the cuisine of post-1965 immigrants. For masala dosa and other South Asian fare there's the Mahatma Gandhi District along Hillcroft Avenue. Or one could seek out the cuisine of East Asia in Chinatown along Bellaire—perhaps visiting the purveyor of much-celebrated spicy central Chinese grub at Mala Sichuan Bistro. Or, in the same shopping center, stop in at Don Cafe

Sandwich, where you're liable to hear a Vietnamese cashier call out an order number in Spanish for a Latino patron while you wait for your own unbeatable and considerably spicy BBQ pork *banh mi*. And those are just the big ones—Houston also has the array of cuisines available in any major American city.

And then, of course, there's the eight-hundred-pound burrito in the room: Tex-Mex.

Tex-Mex shares much in common with Mexican food, defining differences being primarily the heavy use of shredded jack or cheddar cheese rather than *queso fresco*, as is more common south of the Rio Grande; heavy use of cumin, an old-world spice that comes to Texas by way of Spanish immigrants from the Canary Islands, who got it from North Africans; and the use of meat, often beef, in gravies and sauces, as in the Tex-Mex classic chili con carne, rather than sauces more common in Mexico with pure vegetable constituents, like ancho chilies and *guajillo* chilies. Tex-Mex is not a blend of Texan and Mexican food so much as it is the cuisine of the cowboy country of northern Mexico, of which Texas was once the northwesternmost extreme. In that sense Tex-Mex isn't, as the name suggests, a fusion cuisine but the original cuisine of the Tejanos, the first nonindigenous Texans. And if Tex-Mex is the most Texan food, and Houston is the most Texan city, then the most Texan restaurant is Houston's favorite, the Original Ninfa's on Navigation, where, in the words of head chef Alex Padilla, they've "got the best Tex-Mex food since Texas was in Mexico."

The restaurant's odd name—the Original Ninfa's on Navigation—comes from the fact that there were at one time more than two dozen Ninfa's in and around Houston. Today there are a handful of franchises with the name under different ownership, but the original—the community pillar that Houstonians will unfailingly insist you visit lest you stray to a knock-off Ninfa's—is the one on

Navigation. And just in case you get confused, on the wall near the entrance to the Original Ninfa's on Navigation is a mural that says, THERE'S ONLY ONE ORIGINAL NINFA'S AND THIS IS IT.

Mexican American Maria Ninfa Rodriguez Laurenzo—known affectionately as Mama Ninfa—grew up in the Rio Grande Valley in southern Texas. She married an Italian American man, and in 1949 they started a pizza dough and tortilla shop in a garage attached to their small house in Houston's Latino East End. In 1973, following the death of her husband, Mama Ninfa opened a small restaurant in the same location, where she served high-quality Tex-Mex. One thing Ninfa's was—and remains—known for was fajitas. Once a simple dish of cheap cuts of meat doled out to Mexican cowhands, fajitas made use of finer cuts with better spices in Mama Ninfa's hands. Today under the leadership of Alex Padilla, Ninfa's continues to win awards for its fajitas and for its salsa, which is what I really came to check out.

Alex Padilla was born in San Pedro Sula, Honduras, but at ten years old he moved with his family to Houston, where his mother worked at Ninfa's as a dishwasher and line cook. Padilla grew up and moved to northern California, where he attended culinary school at the City College of San Francisco—"because I couldn't afford to go to one of those fancy schools." There he came under the mentorship of the James Beard Award–winning chef Nancy Oakes and developed a trade in cooking French and Californian cuisine in the Bay Area.

Meanwhile, back in Houston, Mama Ninfa passed away in 2001, and her heirs sold the restaurant. The new ownership learned of Padilla and invited him to come back and run Ninfa's as head chef. "I said I'll do it, but it's going to be a challenge," he told me. "I like good ingredients. I need olive oil, kosher salt. Good product, no shortcuts. Fresh product, fresh meat. He said, 'Wonderful, that's what I want for Ninfa's.' Ten years later here we are."

With Padilla at the helm, Ninfa's remains a fabulous restaurant, still serving top-notch Tex-Mex with unpretentious charm. Among Ninfa's many excellent menu items are its two award-winning fresh salsas: a red one of roasted tomato, *chile de arbol,* jalapeño, garlic, cilantro, and salt; and a peculiar green one of avocado, tomatillo, green tomato, cilantro, onion, jalapeño, and sour cream. I asked Padilla to explain the theory behind the second of these—a light, balanced, and subtly creamy salsa the color of baby plants first sprouting from the soil—to get a better understanding of how a chef thinks about cooking with capsaicin.

"Most of the flavors, when the food is fresh, there is no secret," he said. "The secret here is to find the perfect balance between the spicy and the acidity in the tomatoes to make a good salsa."

Balance is essential to cooking, so fundamental it's easy to miss if you're not looking for it—it's the magic of ketchup (sweet) meeting a french fry (salty), or coffee (bitter) meeting a donut (really sweet). This pairing of the five main elements of taste—bitter, sour, salty, sweet, and umami (the subtle earthiness that makes soy sauce soy sauce and not salt sauce)—to achieve a sense of completeness and stability in a dish is what much of cooking is all about.

Though spicy isn't really one of the five major tastes—since it's actually a pain sensation—balance applies when using chilies too. Salsa is an exercise in balance between the spiciness of chilies and the acidity (sourness) of tomatoes, which has the effect of moderating the burn of capsaicin. In Padilla's green salsa, the fat in the avocados and sour cream has a similar grounding effect on the finished product. In chili con carne the cook is essentially building a stew with a grab bag of ingredients balanced against the chilies' burn. It should now be obvious why spicy *arrabbiata* in Italian cooking is a tomato-based sauce. And the entire edifice of classical Chinese Sichuan cuisine is largely built around the idea of balance—or *ma la* in

Chinese, translated as "numbing-hot"—with the numbing effect of Sichuan peppercorns balanced against the heat-pain of chilies.

Annie Rupani practices the subtle art of balance in her work as a chocolatier at her upscale chocolate shop Cacao & Cardamom in west Houston. Born in Karachi, Pakistan, and raised in Sugar Land, a Houston suburb, Rupani embodies the cosmopolitan transformation that has changed the face of her city over the past several decades. As a Pakistani American she grew up eating plenty of spicy food, but for inspiration as a chocolatier in search of balance Rupani often looks to the first cultures that had access to cacao, Mesoamericans, who also happen to be some of the first humans to eat chilies. At her shop, Rupani sells a pyramid-shaped chocolate with a crisp shell surrounding a ganache of dark chocolate infused with chipotle and adobe sauce (which, as it happens, is itself a kind of hot sauce, balancing chilies and other spices with vinegar). She also sells a spicy blend of chocolate, cinnamon, cloves, vanilla, and chipotle and ancho chilies hardened around a stick and designed to be steeped in steaming milk to produce a creamy, spicy hot chocolate that balances the chilies' heat against the cooling effect of milk. Rupani's is an updated—and undoubtedly tastier—version of an austere drink of chocolate, chilies, and vanilla imbibed in ancient Mesoamerica. "It wasn't a glamorous hot chocolate drink," Rupani told me. "It was this bitter, spicy drink that was supposed to be the food from God. It was like a ritual."

Bottled hot sauce is a consequence of this quest for balance, in most cases between the spiciness of chilies, the acidity of vinegar, and the saltiness of salt that together are the primary ingredients in most hot sauces.

All condiments ultimately exist to allow diners to safely customize a dish to achieve balance for themselves with less risk of ruining the meal. What makes hot sauce so wonderful as a table condiment compared with dried chili flakes or even raw chili is the fact that a bottle of hot sauce is, in the end, a sophisticated capsaicin vector finely tuned for balance. A chef will typically make the capsaicin content of a dish rather low (especially a chef cooking for a group, like at a family dinner), leaving chiliheads to add heat themselves to their own specifications. Hot sauce combines elements of taste in such a way that someone who is not a chef is less likely to accidentally ruin his enchiladas than he would be if simply handed a bowl of pureed jalapeño. The condiment thus exists to empower the diner more than the chef. That said hot sauce will at times show up in a recipe—Padilla adds Cholula to his ceviche at Ninfa's, for example, and Tabasco to his Bloody Marys. But "on those two sauces it's the vinegar that I'm really looking for. They'll give me the perfect acidity that I need in my fish," he told me. "The key ingredient in one of those bottled sauces is always going to be the vinegar."

Whether you're using fresh chilies, cooked chilies, or bottled hot sauce, cooking with capsaicin is probably a good idea, and not just because spicy food tastes good. A major study published in 2015 analyzing health outcomes for half a million Chinese adults found that "spicy food consumption showed highly consistent inverse associations with total mortality among both men and women after adjustment for other known or potential risk factors." In other words, the study suggests spicy food saves lives—people who ate spicy food every day or almost every day showed a 14 percent decrease in mortality compared with those who ate spicy less than once a week. In the study, consumption of capsaicin was even associated with decreases in the risk of death from specific ailments, including cancer, ischemic heart diseases, and respiratory diseases. Researchers found the effect most pronounced in those who consumed fresh chilies, but it held true for dried chilies, chili sauce, and chili oil too. More work needs to be done before science can speak authoritatively on the issue, but the China study squares with the results observed by New Zealand scientist Dr. David Popovich, whose lab experiments have found that applying capsaicin to cancer cells appears to reduce their growth.

And though raw chilies enjoy all the health benefits of being raw vegetables, even crushed, minced, pressed, and pulped—even bottled—chilies deliver their health-reinforcing attributes. "Pungent peppers are a cocktail of bioactive compounds," researcher José de Jesús Ornelas-Paz put it to *Time* in 2015. "Blending, cutting and cooking improve the release of [these compounds] from pepper tissue, increasing the amount available for absorption."

In fact, when it comes to capsaicin you're better off eating it with some fat. Since capsaicin is fat soluble, more of it is absorbed into the body when it's paired with a little oil or milk chocolate or avocado . . . Delicious, healthy, and healthier when consumed with fat—how's that for a miracle food?

7

CASHING IN
ON CAPSAICIN

It is, simply, the heavy metal of food.
—Guns N' Roses guitarist Ron "Bumblefoot" Thal

In late April 2014, Dane Wilcox started a conversation thread on the popular website Reddit to ask if anyone wanted a small sample of his home-brewed five-pepper-blend hot sauce. He hoped, if he was lucky, to ship a few hundred samples.

A full-time IT consultant and part-time chilihead, Wilcox had been unsatisfied with the hot sauce available at his local grocery store, and in 2012 he made his first batch of hot sauce out of peppers culled from a few plants grown in the garden of his Portland, Oregon, backyard. He tweaked the recipe over the following year before settling on a blend of habanero, red and green jalapeños, serranos, and Thai chilies, plus citrus, onions, garlic, and carrots for sweetness. Family and friends were so enthusiastic about the sauce he'd perfected for himself that he quickly ran out of it. Wilcox sensed the piquant whiff of opportunity.

He hoped he might make a few bucks by selling the hot sauce that his friends and family had so willingly tested for free, so he decided to launch a crowdfunding campaign on the website Kickstarter to raise money for the effort. He aimed to put together $5,500 in small donations to buy ingredients and materials for the first commercial run of FYM Hot Sauce. But no one—except his chilihead friends and family—had tried the stuff, so, to pique interest, he decided he'd send out tiny sample bottles to Reddit users. Clocking about 150 million page views every month, Reddit is on solid ground when it calls itself "the front page of the internet," but Wilcox figured he'd get at most a few hundred interested people. He'd then use their testimonials as advertising copy for the Kickstarter campaign.

After shipping about two thousand samples Wilcox had to stop—in a prelude for what was to come, Reddit users interested in his free samples had quickly cleaned him fresh out of ingredients. When he finally launched the Kickstarter campaign, it was mere minutes before he had blown through his initial fundraising goal of $5,500 to get his humble hot sauce idea off the ground. By the end of the campaign he'd raked in more than $60,000. He'd promised to send out hot sauce to anyone who donated more than five dollars, and he was suddenly in way over his head.

"It was so fast. It was a very surreal experience," Wilcox recalled later. "It was way beyond what I was prepared for. A lot of people actually complained on Kickstarter because of that."

His initial planned run of about a thousand pounds of hot sauce had expanded to more than ten thousand pounds; he knows that because the weight of his production run exceeded the carrying capacity of the truck he first tried to load it on.

"When it started going way past that, I was like 'I need to get a new place to make all that hot sauce,'" he said. "I didn't have a plan to go that high. It was slightly overwhelming, but I just did my best and it worked out I think." After some delays and fits and starts resulting from a load of orders that vastly exceeded his capacity in the beginning, things settled down. Eventually he outsourced the farming of his ingredients to area farms and increased his production capacity.

Today Wilcox keeps a few loyal clients in his IT consulting business but has largely retired from that to focus exclusively on FYM Hot Sauce production. He's a one-man operation—with occasional help from his family when things get out of hand—churning out batches of about twelve hundred bottles of FYM Hot Sauce at a time, all still made by hand, to meet demand he says comes in waves. All orders come in through his website, FYMHotSauce.rocks. "My biggest problem at the moment is I'm not in any stores yet," he told me. "I've talked to stores, but actually getting into stores is quite difficult, a lot harder than I anticipated."

Reddit is an unforgiving free market of ideas, and discussion threads become popular for one reason alone: because people are excited about them. Clearly, Wilcox had tapped into a hot sauce fever simmering in American society.

From humble origins as a staple in some ethnic and regional cuisines—primarily in the Southwest and in southern Louisiana—America's hot sauce industry has erupted onto the food scene, far outpacing market growth of other condiments. Using data from the market analyst group Euromonitor, the financial news site Quartz found that between 2000 and 2013, the US hot sauce market grew 150 percent, substantially more than the growth in BBQ sauce, ketchup, mayonnaise, and mustard combined. The business intelligence firm IBISWorld found that between 2009 and 2014, revenue in the US hot sauce industry grew 3.6 percent a year to a more than $1 billion industry today. It projects that rate of growth increasing to 4.7 percent from 2014 to 2019.

Over the long term, the current red-hot pace of growth in the hot sauce market is projected to cool somewhat.

"As the market grows, it's going to mature to some extent," Euromonitor Senior Food Analyst Jared Koerten told me. That's economist lingo for a market that has reached supply-demand equilibrium and isn't getting disrupted by innovation (like, the opposite of the cell phone industry, basically). "It's going to be harder to sustain these growth rates."

Even so, Koerten says, growth is not expected to stop or slow significantly anytime in the foreseeable future. "These sauces are really popular with a lot of younger consumers," he said. "A lot of millennials are ditching traditional condiments. Their purchasing power is only going to go up, and they're going to become more important as their purchasing power increases."

As we established in an earlier chapter, part of hot sauce's growth spurt in the United States can be attributed to the growth in absolute terms of the number of immigrants from spicy food–loving cultures. There's also the effect of changing American palates and the millennial crowd Koerten points to as the engine of hot sauce growth. And while American tastes have become more cosmopolitan and more amenable to spicy cuisine overall, when it comes to mainstreaming spicy food, bottled hot sauce has an important advantage over dishes like curry that are cooked to be spicy through and through: with hot sauce, you have control over how much capsaicin ends up on your own plate. Hot sauce has not only benefited from the sudden popularity of spicy cuisines but also helped spicy cuisine along by being a safe entry point for people unaccustomed to chilies.

Dave Dewitt, the "Pope of Peppers" and organizer of Albuquerque's National Fiery Foods & Barbecue Show, which bills itself as the largest spicy foods trade show on earth, sees current trends continuing well into the future.

"When I first got into the business, people were telling me this is just a fad. And I would say, 'This has been a fad for several thousand years.' It's not going to go away—it's just going to get bigger and bigger and bigger," he told me. "You never hear anybody say, 'I used to eat hot and spicy. Now I'm back to bland.'"

The hot sauce industry has been affected primarily in two directions as a result of this breakaway growth in popularity.

First, the increase in demand among young consumers, and among Americans in general with more adventurous palates, has led hot sauce producers to create niche products. Manufacturers have "diversified the heat level of their offerings, creating extra-spicy sauces for fans and daredevils, as well as more mild and unusually flavored offerings, with additives such as chipotle, wasabi, horseradish, mango and chocolate," IBISWorld reports.

Second, when compared with other condiments, the hot sauce industry also benefited in a peculiar way by the economic downturn of the late 2000s. Like nearly the entire economy, the industry took a hit in the downturn; however, "hot sauce producers were barely burned by the recession due to the industry's wide array of affordable products that many consumers view as affordable luxuries," says IBISWorld. Able to remain simple and affordable on the one hand and turn artisanal on the other, the people's condiment remains resilient as ever.

The increased demand for variety in hot sauces has been a boon for smaller niche players, making the last five years or so a great time for an entrepreneurial person to get into the hot sauce business.

I met Ryan Keller, owner and maker of Joshua Tree Organics High Desert Hot Sauce, at his house, which is perched alone atop a small and lonely mountain in the high desert outside Joshua Tree, California. We had a good laugh after I narrowly stopped my borrowed Jeep from rolling unmanned down the mountainside; then he showed me around the property before we sat down to chat over pita bread, dumplings, and his unusual hot sauce.

Keller grew up in SoHo in downtown Manhattan in the 1980s and '90s. In 2007 he graduated from Brown University with degrees in economics and German. Like many in the class of 2007, he watched the global economy go to pieces as he was supposed to be embarking on a career and used the moment of mayhem to do something different. He moved to Berlin, worked at a small-time fashion magazine until it shut down, and then started renting out his apartment on the website Airbnb, a service that was fairly new at the time. Eventually he was running eight Airbnb apartments in Germany and living out of a duffel bag as he shuttled among them. When they were all full, he'd head to the airport and book a ticket. "I'd be on the way to the airport booking a flight to, you know, Málaga. It was just this absurd existence," he said.

"Kind of like rock stardom," I offered.

"It was rock stardom but without the entourage," he said. "Or the music."

Keller took random trips all over Europe and beyond—Italy, Russia, Iceland, Egypt, Turkey, Morocco. "The pitfall is that I was always by myself," he said. "You'd be on a Portuguese island off the coast of Africa and everyone there is on their once-a-year vacation and you're there on a Thursday. I started to get a little jaded by it."

Keller left Europe, moved back to the States, and bought a cheap, run-down property near Joshua Tree National Park. He fixed the place up and then started letting it out on Airbnb. When we met, he'd just finished doing the same thing with a second property, his lonely house on the mountain. In his spare time he decided to launch a hot sauce.

As a seasonal allergy sufferer, Keller had been a hot sauce lover for a long time. About half the year he can't taste anything, but at least with hot sauce he can feel it. "You still get the same pain without any of the taste. I really do enjoy that at least if there's zero taste in my mouth, I feel like there's something happening," he said.

So he cooked up a hot sauce recipe he liked and started bottling it for sale. Unlike most other hot sauces in the Southwest, which tend to be thick cooked-chili purees, his High Desert Hot Sauce is a kind of culinary cultural mélange, with red wine vinegar, lime, garlic, maple syrup, and Thai chilies. It's still, as the bottle says, HANDMADE WITH LOVE IN JT, USA, and available online and at a handful of locations in and around Joshua Tree.

Rick Childress, owner of Fairhope Favorites, has been in the foodstuffs business for a decade but only recently started making hot sauce, after he sensed opportunity in the fast-growing market. "This is just one of those fly-by-the-seat-of-your-pants things, making something out of desperation as the snack industry changed," he told me.

I met Childress under a gazebo on the beach at Mobile Bay in Fairhope, Alabama, a small town of sand and alligators, quaint storefronts and sunshine that exudes a carefully cultivated southern charm. The TV show *Hart of Dixie* is set in the fictional town of Bluebell just five make-believe miles from Fairhope. It's the last outpost of southern gentility on the Gulf Coast before the Redneck Riviera, the hundred-mile stretch of stunning white sand beaches pinned between the Gulf of Mexico and the scary part of Florida.

Childress grew up in the 1950s in Albertville, in northeastern Alabama, "on the Sand Mountain," he told me. "Pretty close to where some shine's been made." That may have something to do with his decision to spend years, he says, perfecting the recipe for his crystal-clear Moonshine Hot Sauce.

"I seen this coming, the moonshine deal," he said, referring to the recent explosion in popularity in the United States of all things moonshine. "Some people may call it a fad, but they waited, what, seventy-something years to make it? I think it's gonna be here longer than a fad. I seen 'em popping up these distilleries everywhere, and I thought, well, what would be more neat than a moonshine hot sauce? A clear hot sauce?"

So a crystal-clear hot sauce he made—and, despite having a good though not bold flavor, it is truly clear as a spring-fed mountain stream, or a new jug of zillion proof white lightning. He's also got an extra-hot version that is a bit cloudy, and a Bourbon Hot Sauce, which is yellow owing to its being aged, like bourbon, in oak barrels and which also comes in a bottle labeled HORSE PISS.

In addition to his normal hot sauce offerings, Childress's company sells a grab bag of other "Redneck Essentials," including a Redneck Back & Butt Scratcher (a stick with bottle caps attached rough side out), Nut Scratcher (same but with a walnut also attached), Fisherman's Ruler (on which an inch is a half inch long), Bubble Bath (beans, with a tiny bottle of Tabasco for flavor), Turkey Turds (malt balls), Soap on a Rope (with one side of the bar labeled FACE, the other BUTT), and Cow Patty Soap on a Rope (bar looks like, but isn't, cow excrement). But back to the hot sauce.

"You going to tell me how you get it clear?" I asked him over the soft din of the waves coming off Mobile Bay.

"Well," he laughed, "I'd probably have to take ya out in water over ya head. And one've us'd stay out there."

"Figured as much. I will press no further," I said. "Any other ingredients you can tell me without taking me out in the water?"

"No, it's fine," Childress said. "We might just go out and wade around in it a little bit."

His moonshine hot sauce, I learned without getting so much as a toe wet, is refreshingly simple: garlic extract, onion extract, cayenne extract, and vinegar. It's spicy with clean flavors, making it a great hot sauce to keep on hand to spice up a dish without overpowering its other constituents. But the clarity of the sauce is about more than an homage to moonshine or an effort to get a clean and simple capsaicin vector.

"From the marketing standpoint," Childress confessed, "when we walk into a store that's got a hot sauce section, if they got one brand or five hundred, most of 'em are red to orange. So you put a total clear one up there and your eyes are going to automatically go to that one." Childress may talk like a good ol' boy, and he does a good job of cultivating a homespun, small-batch image, but his marketing prowess speaks for itself. Moonshine Hot Sauce is available online, in specialty shops throughout the South, and, most crucially, at Bass Pro Shops—that redneck consulate in cities across the country, rural America's Disneyland, and the outdoorsman's number one indoor destination. He ain't doing bad at all.

The hot sauce boom has trickle-down effects, of course. Depending on its scale any given hot sauce might provide jobs for bottlers, designers, truckers, marketers, and others. But one group every hot sauce of any notable size employs by the very nature of the product is farmers.

In the late eighteenth century, on what was then the American frontier—far-flung places like western Pennsylvania—farmers liked to distill their excess grain into whiskey. Compared with harvested grain, the resulting spirit was compact, easily transportable, and for all intents and purposes unspoilable, making it useful as a medium of exchange, like a kind of drinkable currency on the cash-poor frontier. Farmers way out in the boonies had to transport their produce over mountain ranges and through thick woods to get to the cities and markets of the more densely populated east, and to be able to process their crop into something smaller, more durable, and more valuable was an attractive proposition indeed. So attractive that when the newly formed government of the United States levied a tax on distilled spirits—which, for obvious reasons, disproportionately targeted frontier farmers—the farmers rose up in rebellion, tarring and feathering tax collectors and taking up arms against the sprightly young government in what is known in the history books as the Whiskey Rebellion.

I'm not suggesting that hot sauce makers are on the cusp of violent insurrection against the state, but the circumstances that led to the Whiskey Rebellion help illustrate one aspect of hot sauce production that is particularly attractive to chili growers. The chili itself is a rather compact little plant, packing quite the proverbial punch for its size. And the sooner growers can turn the plant into a bottle of hot sauce the better—sealed and steeped in vinegar, like whiskey it won't spoil for a very, very long time. Because it's relatively simple to process, hot sauce is a great value-added product to make right on the farm. Hot sauces produced on the farm tend to be less processed, thick and refreshingly chunky blends in which you can feel and taste the vegetable matter, like those from Hillcrest Farm outside the tiny town of Lillian, near the Gulf Coast in Alabama. Hillcrest produces a small-batch jalapeño and habanero hot sauce called Jala-Haba and a fabulous small-batch, sweet-hot, chunky hot sauce called Ha Cha Cha. It's sold at only a few places around Lillian and at Native Cafe, in Pensacola Beach, Florida. (Try it with Native Cafe's spicy Angry Native Burger. Or the Classic Eggs Benedict. Or really anything else on the menu. Sorry in advance to the purists out there, but it pairs well with ketchup.)

Or take Scrumptious Pantry out of Chicago, Illinois, which brings to market hot sauces made with heirloom chilies, like chiltepin chilies and Beaver Dam chilies, and other ingredients procured from farmers around the Midwest. The company partners with Co-Op Sauce, which bottles and sells handcrafted, small-batch hot sauce to support Co-Op Image, a free arts and entrepreneurship education program for Chicago youth. Farmers loom so large in the Scrumptious Pantry's conception of itself that its hot sauces are bottled with charming color illustrations of the farmers who grow the produce that goes into their sauces.

Chili farming is particularly attractive for the nascent urban farming movement, in which industrious green thumbs are converting smaller urban spaces like empty lots and rooftops into working farms—for instance, Brooklyn Grange, in New York City, the world's largest commercial rooftop farm. The Grange's sweet and savory Brooklyn Grange Rooftop Hot Sauce is produced from seed to bottle with chilies and spices grown on its Red Hook rooftop. And Brooklyn Grange isn't an anomaly, even in America's biggest, baddest, most compact city.

Thanks to some other enterprising farmers in New York, the Bronx is burning again—but this time in a good way. Small Axe Peppers, a for-profit company started in 2014 with seed money from two housing developers in the Bronx, partnered with GrowNYC to support small-scale community gardens by producing a hot sauce. New York City restaurateur King Phojanakong cooked up a recipe including apple cider vinegar, garlic, onion, salt, and serrano peppers, and the Bronx Greenmarket Hot Sauce was born. The serranos are grown in gardens in the Bronx that are tended by young people in the community, who are paid for their farm labor. The harvest is supplemented as needed from farms upstate.

At the other end of the manufacturing process from farms are retailers, like Heatonist, "purveyors of fine hot sauces," a boutique hot sauce shop that opened to great fanfare in Greenpoint, Brooklyn, in 2015.

I asked shop owner Noah Chaimberg, a New Yorker by way of Montreal, how he came to be a self-proclaimed hot sauce sommelier in Brooklyn.

"Well, one day I was walking down the street and everything was pretty normal," he told me. "I was hungry and going to get a taco at the taco truck, and out of nowhere this car went through a light, and a Tabasco truck was coming and just swerved and missed him, and I was covered in a shower of hot sauce. When I woke up in the hospital months later—"

"OK. Now tell me something true."

"Somebody challenged me to use that one time for real," he said.

"I like it," I said, motioning to get on with the real story.

"We needed a place in New York where you could come to discover new and interesting hot sauces. It just didn't exist. There was nothing—no place you could go to taste, but also no place that had this variety of flavors that's out there these days. So that's what really led to this wanting to stand on that side of the counter, just wanting to be able to have access to the variety that exists." His shop, the Heatonist, carries a small but carefully curated selection of hot sauces from around the United States. What it doesn't carry, uniquely among hot sauce sellers, are hot sauces with xanthan gum, a thickening agent used in everything from makeup to concrete to a vast array of table sauces, hot or otherwise—you probably eat it on a weekly if not daily basis. There's no good evidence that xanthan gum itself is bad for you, and it's a legal food additive around the world, though the Federal Drug Administration did recommend manufacturing process improvements after it found that xanthan gum can occasionally be contaminated by endotoxins, which can make you sick.

"People say it's all natural, xanthan gum. It was invented by scientists in the '50s, so, like, how all-natural is all natural?" Noah said. That's sort of true. It was more discovered than invented; xanthan gum is a slime excreted by bacteria. "I think there's about 85 or 90 percent of hot sauces off the table for us. But what we do carry is all, you know, the real, handcrafted, best stuff. The stuff that you'd pick if you were going to make hot sauce at home. You wouldn't be reaching for xanthan gum or the capsaicin extract, you'd be reaching for peppers and going to the markets for ingredients."

The xanthan gum prohibition does substantially limit the Heatonist's hot sauce selection—it's really pretty small—but necessity, as they say, is the mother of invention. What sauces they do have are truly unique, excellent across the board, and made with handcrafted care, like Bravado Spice Co.'s Ghost Pepper and Blueberry Hot Sauce, Marshall's Haute Sauce's Habañero and Carrot Curry, and Torchbearer Sauce's Zombie Apocalypse Sauce. Like at a hot sauce festival, you can taste sauces before you buy them—an innovation one hopes catches on among other hot sauce vendors—making Heatonist not merely a place to shop but a destination unto itself for chiliheads living in or visiting the Big Apple.

While the tasting room is a nice touch, a shop that sells specialty hot sauce is, of course, no innovation at all. Such shops exist in cities all over the United States: Light My Fire in Los Angeles, iBurn in Houston, Pepper Palace in New Orleans, and Tears of Joy Sauces in Austin, to name just a few.

Francesca Kay's hot sauce shop, the Chile Addict in Albuquerque, New Mexico, has been slinging hot sauce and chili-related items for more than thirty years. She's seen the hot sauce scene change in that time.

"It's changed a lot since 9/11," she told me, "because people are only allowed to take three ounces of fluid now [through airport security], of hot sauce. They used to come and just get a bunch of hot sauce, bunch of stuff, wrap it and take it. Now they can't do that."

I heard the same story from hot sauce sellers across the United States—though not the cashier at Light My Fire, who might have warned me before loading me up with a dozen-some-odd bottles of hot sauce that would get me in hot water with the TSA. By prohibiting people from bringing liquids in carry-on luggage, the post–September 11, 2001, airport security changes took a noticeable bite out of sales from boutique brick-and-mortar stores. Major national and international brands (Tabasco et al.) are largely unaffected, but local and regional hot sauces that can't be found at your chain grocery store have felt it. This is especially true now that hot sauce fiends seeking new and unique ways to burn themselves have access to a profusion of hot-sauce-of-the-month-type groups online, like Hot Sauce Club at hotsauce.club. (The first rule of Hot Sauce Club is you do not talk about Hot Sauce Club. If you've seen the movie *Fight Club*, you already know the second rule of Hot Sauce Club.)

The overarching trend in hot sauce, Kay says, has been toward ever-spicier sauces.

"The trend has gone to the hotter the better. The people who eat hot sauce want it really hot," she told me. "To show off."

In tandem with this trend toward ever-hotter sauces, new hot sauce festivals pop up around the country where chiliheads can taste new sauces and take on hot sauce challenges, like CaJohn's "Execution Station," where a vendor will guide you (excruciatingly slowly) through a tasting of eight or so hot sauces that toward the end get up north of 1 million SHU. If you make it to the end, you get an I Survived beer koozie—I've got one to prove it—plus bragging rights. In just the last few years numerous new hot sauce festivals have been born around the United States, including the NYC Hot Sauce Expo, the Louisiana Hot Sauce Expo, the Chicago Hot Sauce Fest, and the California Hot Sauce Expo.

Idiotic machismo has always been a thing, granted, but just twenty years ago these sorts of extreme hot sauce challenges didn't really exist, because hot sauces were by and large not very spicy. The maker of Dave's Insanity Sauce, Dave Hirschkop, was banned in the mid-1990s from the National Fiery Foods & Barbecue Show for doling out samples of his hot sauce that were so spicy they made people sick. But Dave's Insanity Sauce rates only about 180,000 SHU. Today at the NYC Hot Sauce Expo, which had its first year in 2013, any idiot (like yours truly) can stumble over to the Voodoo Chile booth and into a multimillion-Scoville collision with scorpion pepper tincture.

The shift toward spicier sauces is a result of changing tastes, not technology. Humans have been able to create extremely high concentrations of capsaicin—like the extracts and tinctures used in many of the hottest hot sauces—since at least the 1960s, when modern pepper spray was invented. (It was later issued to postal workers for use as a dog repellant.) After Dave's Insanity Sauce opened the superspiciness floodgates, things changed fast. In 1994 the world encountered a chili hotter than anything known before, the half a million–SHU Red Savina, a habanero cultivar bred in California. In 2007 the Red Savina was displaced by the million-SHU Bhut Jolokia, also known as the ghost pepper, an Indian chili. In 2012 Dr. Paul Bosland at the Chile Pepper Institute identified the scorpion pepper, from Trinidad and Tobago, as the hottest known cultivar, with an average of 1.2 million SHU. In 2013 the *Guinness Book of World Records* declared a cultivar hybridized by Ed Currie at his farm/lab in South Carolina, the on-average 1.5 million-SHU Carolina reaper, to be the hottest chili on earth.

The rapid climb in chili spiciness indicates a general interest in finding or making spicier chilies, but superhot chilies aren't necessary to make an extract of the kind used to make the really spicy sauces—most of those are made with capsaicin harvested from plain old cayenne peppers, because they're cheap, or from synthetic capsaicin. Blair's Sauces and Snacks out of New Jersey effectively ended the race to the hottest sauce when it started releasing its utterly pointless

16 million SHU "hot sauce," if you can call it that—16,000,000 SHU is pure capsaicin.

No one is better poised to help us understand how hot sauce in America got to where it is today than John Hard, a former fire protection engineer from Columbus, Ohio, who grew up in what he describes as the "eatin' potatoes Midwest." In the 1970s, Hard began traveling to southern Louisiana for fire protection work with the oil industry and on those trips encountered truly spicy food for the first time. He fell in love with Cajun country and its fiery cuisine and in time earned himself a nickname, a portmanteau of Cajun and his first name: CaJohn. He launched a website and eventually his own line of hot sauces under that name and has become easily one of the most respected and beloved people in the industry. More than once I've heard other hot sauce makers refer to him as "the godfather," a title bestowed not because of a penchant for making unrefusable offers but for his renowned magnanimity and willingness to help newbie hot sauce makers get started, like Ron "Bumblefoot" Thal, the former Guns N' Roses guitarist who launched his own line of Bumblefoot hot sauces with CaJohn's help.

Today CaJohn laments how secretive the industry has become since the 1990s, when makers weren't so guarded about their recipes (very few of which are really all that complicated anyway) and an air of openness held between hot sauce producers. But he doesn't regret the immense growth in the market and surely not the wild success his hot sauces have had since.

"We went through a thing in the '90s," CaJohn told me. "First it was the eating healthier kick. You were taking the fats out of the diet. You take the fats out, you generally take the flavor out. If you put spices or hot sauce back into it, you're not getting any of the fats but you're getting plenty of flavor. The number two thing is the television channel Food Network. People started watching TV, people stopped trying to find the store brand products and started looking for the products they had on the TV, and it just made people—I think we went through a generation where people were afraid to cook, and I think food TV made it very approachable and turned them onto products other than what was on the shelves."

"But the industry has really kicked off in the last several years," I said. "What's going on?"

"Well, I have a theory on that," CaJohn said. "And I call it: We're riding the Sriracha Wave."

Historically hot sauces with a national presence in the United States have been the salty, vinegary, thin sauces, like Tabasco. "Now, Sriracha's different," he said. "It's sweet, it's garlicky, it's thick, and it's made with jalapeños, so it's not as sharp. I think it's turned on a whole new group of people, whether you want to call them the hipsters or whatever, but it's turned a whole bunch of new people to the idea that hot sauce is not Tabasco or Frank's RedHot."

Compared with other industries, hot sauce production has a low degree of concentration, with the four biggest firms controlling only about 39 percent of revenue in the industry overall as of 2014, the rest going to small-scale, specialty producers. But even some of the biggest national brands with the deepest roots in American culture aren't exactly industry heavyweights. Bruce Food Corporation out of New Iberia, Louisiana, since 1928, maker of Louisiana Hot Sauce, can lay claim to only 3.1 percent of the market. TW Garner Food Company, which makes Texas Pete Hot Sauce out of Winston-Salem, North Carolina, has only about 3.3 percent of the market cornered. Even Reckitt Benckiser Group PLC, owner of the storied Frank's RedHot, which has been produced and bottled for sale in Springfield, Missouri, since 1920 and is the second-best-selling hot sauce in America, controls only 12.3 percent of the market.

With hot sauce labeled in twenty-two languages* and sold in more than 165 countries, annual revenue believed to be more than $200 million, and an estimated 19 percent of the hot sauce market under its thumb, McIlhenny Company's Tabasco Pepper Sauce is the unrivaled Goliath in the hot sauce universe. The Tabasco bottle, small and clear with its famous red cap, is iconic. The family-owned firm is famously guarded and will not give out or even confirm information about revenue, profit margins, or really anything else about its finances, but there is simply no way around the fact that Tabasco reigns supreme. No other company can say it is the maker of the official hot sauce of Air Force One. (Since the George H. W. Bush administration they have labeled bottles especially for the White House entourage.) Tabasco sells extremely well in the United States, but the company's heady growth in recent years—revenue was estimated to be "just" $155 million in 2008—has, analysts believe, been driven largely by exports. Japan is the world's biggest importer of Tabasco, owing perhaps to the substantial American military presence there after the Second World War or to a heavy advertising campaign in the 1950s and 1960s that paired Tabasco with pasta and pizza, which were then being introduced to the country, or both.

In the parlance of trend watchers, Tabasco is undoubtedly hot, but it's also the industry standard, like Coca-Cola, the Old Reliable you can count on whether at a Milwaukee Chipotle or a Dubai hotel. Tabasco is not the hottest thing on the hot sauce scene these days. For that we must look to another iconic bottle—this one with a green cap.

Even if he's famously tight-lipped, the rough outlines of the life story of the "unsurpassable genius" David Tran, as his company's

---

* They are, according to CEO Tony Simmons: Arabic, Chinese, Cyrillic, Danish, Dutch, English, Finnish, Flemish, French, French-Canadian, Greek, Italian, Japanese, Korean, Spanish, Norwegian, Swedish, Swiss, Portuguese, Brazilian Portuguese, German, and Austrian.

history on its website refers to him, are well known by now. In 1978, while hundreds of thousands of South Vietnamese were being executed and put to hard labor at reeducation camps in the years after the fall of Saigon, a former officer in the army of South Vietnam fled the country like thousands of his countrymen. One of the so-called "Vietnamese Boat People," David Tran escaped aboard a Taiwanese cargo ship named *Huey Fong*. He made it to the United States, where he was granted refugee status and settled, at first, in Boston.

Back in Vietnam, Tran had started making hot sauce while working in the kitchen in the army. In 1975 he started producing and selling a hot sauce bottled in recycled glass baby food jars called Pepper Sa-te. (*Sa-te*, or *Sate*, is the generic term for the oily chili paste in the little trays on the tables at Vietnamese restaurants.) He hoped to revive his chili sauce business in the United States but found that Boston isn't exactly chili-growing country. So he moved to Southern California, where he knew he could get fresh chilies. There he concocted his own spin on a hot sauce he had enjoyed in Southeast Asia, specifically as a sauce to pair with the brothy Vietnamese soup called *pho*. Distributing his hot sauce himself out of a blue van, he sold to Asian restaurants in L.A.'s Chinatown, near where his first production facility was located, and elsewhere in California, from San Diego to San Francisco. In time he would start a company and name it Huy Fong Foods, in honor of the boat that got him out of Indochina. (Tran said *Huy* is the Vietnamese spelling of the same word, *Huey*, in Chinese.) Tran, who is ethnically Chinese, bottled his sauce under a label with a rooster on it, a nod to the fact that he was born in 1945, the year of the rooster in the Chinese zodiac. His sauce is known today by a few monikers: rooster sauce, cock sauce, or most commonly of all by the generic term for the type of sauce it is, Sriracha, a name that is lifted from the coastal town in Thailand, Si Racha, on the Bay of Bangkok. The sauce was supposedly invented

there more than half a century ago by a woman named Thanom
Chakkapak to give to her family and friends.

Chakkapak's sauce, which is sweeter and much less spicy than
Tran's version, can still be purchased under the name Sriraja Panich.
It's hard to find in the United States, but it's one of the most popular
table sauces in Thailand. There are so many different spellings of
Sriracha or *Si Racha* or whatever because all are phonetic approxima-
tions of the name of the town in Thai, a language with an alphabet
all its own that does not correspond directly to English letter sounds.
The correct pronunciation, though, is always "si-ra-cha," with that
first *r* kept silent.

If you are unaware that America is in the grip of a Sriracha
craze—which shows no sign of abating and which we will eventually have to stop calling a craze, unless we're also willing to talk
about America's ketchup craze, mustard craze, and so forth—then I'd
like to hear more about the rock you've been hiding under, because
it sounds like a great napping spot. In 2014 IBISWorld estimated
that Huy Fong Foods cornered 4.2 percent of the hot sauce market,
but my guess is that number has already increased substantially and
will continue to do so. The company does not like to give out sales
numbers, but Huy Fong Foods confirmed to me that rain or shine,
recession or boom time, it has seen "steady growth each year since the
company's inception 35 years ago." A wonderful short documentary
about Sriracha by the filmmaker Griffin Hammond reports that
Huy Fong Foods' sales increase by roughly 20 percent year on year,
which, if true, is a head-spinning growth rate indeed. All this with
zero advertising and without employing even a single salesperson to
go out and solicit business. The product sells itself. Huy Fong Foods'
first factory in Los Angeles was five thousand square feet; in 2013,
Tran's business moved into a 650,000-square-foot facility in Irwin-
dale, a suburb on the outskirts of the Los Angeles metropolitan area.

Part of what makes Sriracha so good is that it plays on the cravings of the caveman inside us all using a trick employed by chefs the world over. In addition to red jalapeños—all sourced from a single Southern California farm that sells its entire crop to Huy Fong Foods—ingredients include xanthan gum, garlic, vinegar, and the two flavors that are the foundation of, like, every secret ingredient ever: salt and sugar.

Huy Fong's Sriracha came of age by word of mouth in the era of social media, and no other sauce commands so many expressions of passionate loyalty. There's the documentary. There's a viral Sriracha-chugging YouTube challenge. There are Sriracha cookbooks. There's a Sriracha festival. There are way more terrible musical odes to Sriracha on the Internet than the world needed. There is Sriracha-themed clothing enough to fill a wardrobe many times over. And there are dozens of Srirachas from other brands now, including one from the titan of the industry, Tabasco, and a shabby, cringe-worthy version from Trader Joe's with packaging that shamelessly rips off Huy Fong Foods' iconic clear plastic bottle, white lettering, and green cap.

IBISWorld's industry analysis makes special note of the fact that Sriracha "is swiftly moving beyond Thai and other Asian restaurants to becoming a staple for pairing with non-Asian cuisines such as pizza and hot dogs." Or "hamburgers, chow mein or on anything," as Huy Fong Foods suggests in the text on its Sriracha bottles. Or, according to a quick and wholly unscientific survey of Sriracha lovers: peanut butter, pickles, peanut butter–pickle–bacon sandwiches, beer, popcorn, Fritos, oysters, avocado, mashed potatoes, steel-cut oatmeal, pineapple, watermelon, maple syrup on pancakes, dark chocolate truffles, donuts, lemonade, in whipped cream for Mexican hot chocolate, in whipped cream on cornbread, or, if you're my dear friend Spencer Livingston-Gainey, who introduced me to Sriracha so many years ago, your very own finger.

Hot sauce lovers everywhere owe a hearty thank-you to David Tran, in gratitude for a wonderful hot sauce, for the "Sriracha wave" that has helped set the industry and innovation within it ablaze, and for what has got to be the greatest hot sauce quip ever quipped, said once by Tran in response to a request that Huy Fong Foods tamp down the heat in its Sriracha: "Hot sauce must be hot. If you don't like it hot, use less. We don't make mayonnaise here."

8

CHICKEN WINGS AND SOUTHERN THINGS

Hot tamales and they're red hot, yes she got 'em for sale
Man don't mess around 'em hot tamales now
Cause they too black bad, if you mess around 'em hot tamales
I'm 'onna upset your backbone, put your kidneys to sleep
I'll due to break away your liver and dare your heart to beat bout my
Hot tamales cause they red hot, yes they got 'em for sale, I mean
Yes, she got 'em for sale.
—ROBERT JOHNSON, "HOT TAMALES"

I shredded a tire doing eighty on the interstate in Upstate New York a few hours outside of Buffalo. After putting on the spare in the median with cars whizzing by feet from my skull, and entertaining horrifying visions of the cost of new shoes for my car, I was, by the time I finally entered Buffalo's hulking postindustrial cityscape, in an agitated state. If you had to pick a city to descend upon in a bad mood, it turns out Buffalo, New York, wouldn't be a bad choice.

I drove straight to the highest rated tire shop I could find with a quick smartphone search, Cleve-Hill Auto & Tire on Main Street. The folks behind the counter were extremely nice. All the other patrons were extremely nice—one of them later recognized me on the street, stopped his car, and just gave me an extra tire he had on hand. For free. In a stroke of bizarre coincidence, directly across the street from Cleve-Hill Auto & Tire was the place I'd traveled all the way up to the northern reaches of America to visit: Anchor Bar, home of the buffalo chicken wing. In Buffalo even coincidences are extremely nice.

A sure way to mark oneself as an outsider in Buffalo—other than being anything less than extremely nice—is to place an order for buffalo chicken wings. For in Buffalo they are not called buffalo chicken wings. When I took up a stool in Anchor Bar, even the pint of Labatt Blue (a Canadian beer with regional reach) I ordered could not camouflage my outsiderness after I ordered a plate of buffalo chicken wings, and it is thanks only to the fact that the bartender and patrons alike were all extremely nice that I was politely set straight rather than laughed out of the bar. Texas toast is still Texas toast in Texas, and California rolls are California rolls in California, but in Buffalo the pattern does not hold. Perhaps because their provenance is held to be so truly and deeply Buffalonian (a real word); because as a snack, meal, and art form they are held in such high esteem by the people of Buffalo; or because they are so revered as one of that frigid city's hottest homegrown innovations, in Buffalo, buffalo wings are called, simply, "wings."

Today Anchor Bar serves up unremarkable pub grub and Italian-American fare, plus a steady cascade of fantastic chicken wings coated in either their famous sauce (hot or cut with butter down to medium or mild) or their spicier "Suicide Sauce," which is not really all that hot and not nearly as good as the traditional stuff. Almost all Buffalo sauce these days is Frank's RedHot cut with butter, but Anchor Bar has its own recipe, which is noticeably if slightly different and, in my estimation, superior. Anchor also makes its own blue cheese dressing, which is very good indeed.

The place is packed with kitsch. Most of it is typical bar stuff—law enforcement patches, license plates, sports ephemera, random motorcycle-related things, including actual motorcycles somehow attached to the ceiling—but there's also a small room off to the side where Anchor Bar gear and bottles of its famous house-made Wing Sauce are sold. Next to the little store stands an unsettling life-size statue of either a leather-skinned old woman or a mummy in a maid's uniform presenting a heaping plate of wings coated in orange sauce with a side of celery and blue cheese. This novelty is often presumed to be the likeness of someone associated with the buffalo wing's creation. It is not. But just outside the front door is a much humbler wooden statue carved in 2006 of a short woman presenting a bowl of wings who is belatedly getting her due: Teressa Bellissimo.

In 1980, on assignment for *The New Yorker*, writer Calvin Trillin set out to document the origins of the buffalo chicken wing. In a shockingly short period of time, the bar snack had grown wildly popular across the region, then the country, and eventually the world, becoming the gateway drug that has since seduced many people (including, to name just two, Graham Connolly of LBI Love Potion and Baron Ambrosia) into the world of spicy food. "Since Buffalo chicken wings were invented less than twenty years ago," Trillin wrote at the time, "I had figured that I would have an easy task compared to, say, a medievalist whose specialty requires him to poke around in thirteenth-century Spain." Trillin, of course, found the task of tracing the origins of even a famed food to be not quite so easy.

His article was published only a few years after the City of Buffalo issued an official proclamation celebrating Anchor Bar co-owner Frank Bellissimo and declaring July 29, 1977, Chicken Wing Day: "WHEREAS, the success of Mr. Bellissimo's tasty experiment in

1964 has grown to the point where thousands of pounds of chicken wings are consumed by Buffalonians in restaurants and taverns throughout our city each week . . ."

The story, as Frank is reported to have consistently told it, is that one day in 1964 a supplier accidentally delivered chicken wings instead of the chicken backs and necks typically used in spaghetti sauce. Frank had the groundbreaking idea to turn the wings, long considered a throwaway part of the bird, into something more dignified than sauce. He asked his wife to do something with the wings, so she chopped them in half, deep fried them, coated them in hot sauce, and presented them with celery and blue cheese salad dressing. Thus the buffalo chicken wing was born.

Frank's son Dom recounted a different origin story to Trillin, in which on one Friday night in 1964 he thought up the idea to make something special to serve at the stroke of midnight to a group of Catholic patrons who'd been spending a lot of money at the bar and who could, once the day clicked over, quit the traditional Catholic Friday diet of fish. He asked his mom to make a meat snack, so she chopped them in half, etcetera, etcetera, and the buffalo chicken wing was born.

Yet another version of the story has Teressa simply improvising a snack for Dom and his friends on a random late evening. You will note that whichever version of the story you prefer, the only real innovator at work is Teressa, making the city's 1977 proclamation lauding Frank's invention a comical if a little unnerving artifact of its time.

But contradictory tales about the origins of buffalo wings at Anchor Bar don't even begin to address the real complexity of the question. Because when it comes to the origins of buffalo chicken wings, we're confronted with what one might call a rock 'n' roll problem; Buddy Holly, the Big Bopper, and Elvis may have taken rock 'n' roll to new heights, but those white rockers by no means invented the genre.

While reporting his buffalo wings story, Trillin met a black man named John Young who claimed it was he who by all rights deserved credit for inventing buffalo wings. Young had grown up in Alabama farm country and moved to Buffalo as a teenager, part of the Great Migration of black southerners out of the American South in the mid twentieth century. Young said he sold the famed dish out of his restaurant called John Young's Wings 'n Things from 1964 until he left Buffalo for Decatur, Illinois, in 1970. "If the Anchor Bar was selling chicken wings, nobody in Buffalo knew it then," Young told Trillin—he'd recently moved back to Buffalo when they spoke. "After I left here, everybody started chicken wings." Young made the very good point to Trillin that for black Americans, eating chicken wings was no innovation at all. Like most poor, rural people, they had been eating chicken wings—a part of the bird generally discarded by the more affluent—for centuries. Young, who served his wings whole (not chopped in half), said he'd invented a tomato-based condiment called mambo sauce, and his innovation was to put the sauce on his breaded-and-fried wings.

Young died in 1998, but in 2013 *Buffalo News* columnist Donn Esmonde used his weekly column to solicit help in tracking down any living relatives, and track them down he did. Esmonde's reporting corroborates much of Young's story, and he even found relatives of Young serving up chicken wings with mambo sauce in Buffalo out of a restaurant called Taste of Soul. Sadly, Taste of Soul has since closed, and if John Young's mambo sauce is available at a wings eatery in Buffalo, I haven't been able to find it, and thus I've never tasted it. But I did find someone who has.

Buffalonian Drew Cerza founded the National Buffalo Wing Festival in 2002. In 2007 celebrity chef Bobby Flay challenged Cerza to a chicken wing cook-off throw-down, lost, and dubbed Cerza the "Wing King." The name stuck, and for good reason. Drew Cerza knows his way around a buffalo wing.

John Young's daughter Lina Brown-Young is in possession of the old mambo sauce recipe and got in touch with Cerza one day. "She made me a batch,'" he told me. "It was sweet. More of a sweeter—but a very good sauce.

"A little spicy," he added.

I'd been unable to get back in touch with Young's relatives myself, and Cerza didn't know how to reconnect with them either.

"I wish there was some way I could get ahold of someone who knew how to make mambo sauce," I said.

"Yeah," he said, empathizing. "They wouldn't give out the recipe either, I'll tell you that."

But I wasn't totally out of luck—John Young's mambo sauce, it seems, may have been a part of a still-living sauce tradition. Esmonde also reported that Young's brother told him Young opened Wings-n-Things after hearing about a successful wing place in Washington, DC. And here, like a goopy sauce left to simmer on the stove, the plot thickens yet.

Mambo sauce is a much-loved homegrown tradition in the chicken joints of Washington, DC, a city where black residents made up as much as two-thirds of the population in the latter half of the twentieth century and only lost racial majority status in 2011. The supersweet, sticky, and tangy ketchup-based sauce is still popular in DC's carryout eateries, especially the sort found in working-class neighborhoods and that have no seating and advertise a dizzying and patternless lineup of foods, like CHINESE, FRIED CHICKEN, SUBS, SEAFOOD, PIZZA. DC residents dispute where the sauce originated, but there seems to be a consensus around its appearance circa the 1960s in the wing shops that were once common all over the nation's now fast-gentrifying capital city, and which still hang on mightily in many neighborhoods. Mambo sauce has a strong cultural association with go-go, a style of music that emerged in DC around the same time, which combines funk with early-stage hip-hop but ditches the electronic beat in favor of natural percussion more like the sound of a busking bucket drummer than a percussionist behind a trap set. Go-go is gussied-up street funk. The mambo sauce–covered chicken wing is its culinary companion.

Anyone trying to nail down anything beyond those bare-bones facts about DC mambo sauce will inevitably run into the same problem, best exemplified by the fact that no one can even agree on what mambo sauce in DC is actually called. It's alternately rendered as mumbo sauce, mombo sauce, mamba sauce, and even mumble sauce. It's sometimes written in different forms at the same restaurant, and that's if it is written down at all. Very often mambo sauce doesn't appear anywhere in writing on a menu. The sauce has obvious similarities with Chinese sweet-and-sour sauce and may have an ancestral linkage therefrom as well, but the clearest ingredient and the common unifying factor among mambo sauces, which vary considerably between different establishments, is ketchup. The problem for a hack on the hot sauce trail is that, varied though they are, most mambo sauces today aren't even a little bit spicy.

After walking by myself to several carryout places in DC in an unsuccessful search for spicy mambo sauce, I enlisted the help of a top-notch journalist friend. One can only stomach so many cloyingly sweet wings before one needs some moral support.

On one summer Sunday my friend and colleague at *Time* magazine Jay Newton-Small joined me on a drive around the vast swath of Washington east of the Anacostia River known to many Washingtonians, incorrectly, simply as Anacostia, which is the name of just one of several neighborhoods on that side of the river. It's a part of

Washington that is today almost exclusively populated by African Americans and is known, not totally unfairly, for a much higher crime rate than the rest of the city. Once the home of Frederick Douglass, it's also one of the oldest neighborhoods in town, with rolling hills that make it the most topographically pleasing part of the city. Built up over the years as a suburb for Washingtonians who commuted to jobs across the river, it's a part of DC with a long and rich working-class history.

I got in Jay's car and we first drove to Harry's Wings-N-Things. I thought it held promise because when I'd called days earlier, the woman who answered the phone said she made her own mambo sauce and then told me—I'm paraphrasing here—to leave her the hell alone. Sadly we found the place closed and drove on. Jay came to a stop at the corner of Alabama Avenue and Martin Luther King Jr. Boulevard.

"You know who would know where to find the best mambo sauce around?" she said, looking across me in the passenger seat and out the window. I followed her gaze to a cop sitting on his motorcycle. The beat cop. Of course. My plan to take advantage of a reporter friend more talented than I was already paying off. I asked the police officer where to find mambo sauce, and he pointed to a building less than fifty feet away.

"Hong Kong Delite Carry Out," he said. "Best mambo sauce in the seventh district."

Inside we were disappointed to find this mambo sauce to be as sweet and unspicy as the rest. But that's not all.

I struck up a conversation with fellow patron Barbara Rogers, a lifelong resident of the District of Columbia who, once I told her what I was up to, told me matter-of-factly that mambo sauce was invented in the 1960s by a former coworker of hers at the Department of Corrections who also ran a place on Georgia Avenue in

Northwest DC across the street from Howard University Hospital called Wings-n-Things.

"Her mambo sauce was different from theirs," Rogers told me. "Hers had a good sweet taste to it. It was more of a barbecue sauce. She gave me the recipe years ago"—my heart skipped a beat—"but I lost it in my storage bin."

"Can you remember any of the ingredients?" I asked.

"I know it's vinegar in it. I know it's hot sauce in it. I know it's ketchup."

"Would you call it spicy?" I asked.

"It was"—she paused—"mild. She made some spicy. Her sauce was the best in town." Rogers said Crystal's, a relatively mild hot sauce, was the one typically used in those mambo sauce concoctions.

It is not easy to find spicy mambo sauce in Washington today. I eventually made it to Harry's Wings-N-Things only to find that its homemade mambo sauce had no detectable bite whatsoever. I did meet a group of teenage girls there who live in the area and who directed me to a Chinese carryout place in Anacostia proper called Good Hope Seafood. There I was delighted to find a house-made mambo sauce that does contain traces of hot sauce, a distant descendant of the spicier mambo sauce of the past. Still, though most people will tell you that hot sauce is a recurring ingredient in mambo sauce, it is very rarely detectable, at least to your average hot sauce fiend. Anyone searching for a classic DC mambo sauce that is in any way spicy is better off ordering a bottle of sweet and spicy online from Capital City Co., which makes and sells a mambo sauce that is—Eureka!—indeed spicy. It is far and away the best mambo sauce I found. In its official company history, Capital City Co. backs up Rogers's account, reporting that mambo sauce was probably invented at the Wings-n-Things near Howard University Hospital.

It's tempting to end our search here, but as the self-styled "Barbecue Whisperer" and head honcho of the popular 'cue website AmazingRibs.com "Meathead" Goldwyn has written, mambo sauce may have an even deeper ancestry. "The original Mumbo sauce was probably a ketchupy barbecue sauce created in Chicago in 1957 by Argia B. Collins Sr.," Goldwyn concludes.

Goldwyn traces the origins of Mumbo sauce—a spelling, remember, that is perfectly accepted in the mambo sauce heartland of DC—to a now-long-gone ribs-and-more joint on the South Side of Chicago called Argia B's Bar-B-Q, where "Mumbo sauce" was bottled for sale as early as 1957. It may have been created, he surmises, under the influence of sauces in nearby Chinatown, like plum sauce and sweet-and-sour sauce, which would help explain its popularity in Chinese carryout storefronts. Argia's became a neighborhood staple famous both for the Q it churned out and for the free victuals it provided to hard-up Chicago civil rights activists in the 1960s. "Whoever needed to be fed, we'd tell them to go to the barbecue house. It was phenomenal. Argia was well-loved," Hazel Thomas, a longtime volunteer with the civil rights group Operation Breadbasket, told a *Chicago Tribune* reporter for Argia Collin's obituary in 2003. "He was a kind, generous person. We ate a lot of barbecue." Argia B's Mumbo sauce can still be bought today both online and at retail outlets primarily in the Chicago area.

And yet our journey is still not at an end. For like John Young, Argia Collins was not a native of the North country but another product of the Great Migration to industrial northern cities out of the agricultural South, where black Americans were reeling under decades of Jim Crow oppression and an economy increasingly stacked against the small farmer. Like Muddy Waters, Earl Hooker, and other musicians who immigrated up river to Chicago, where they gave life to a new urbanized and electrified style of the blues,

Argia Collins migrated to the Windy City after growing up in the Mississippi Delta—in a town called Indianola, to be exact, the home of B. B. King.

When I was a teenager, my grandfather gave me my first guitar, a cherry-red, cheap but sturdy Fender Squier, which I promptly covered with punk rock stickers and, in sharpie, a depressingly short list of every girl's phone number I could get. When I started lessons, I didn't know much about anything, but I'd heard B. B. King, the Ambassador of the Blues, and so the blues is what I first learned to play.

As I was driving out of Buffalo to pay a quick visit to Niagara Falls, I heard the news over the radio that B. B. King had died. At the falls I parked my car and spent a while staring absentmindedly into the crashing field of white water. Then I took a nap, and as the sun went down, I bought a cup of coffee, set a B. B. King anthology playing on the car stereo, and hustled on down south to pay my respects in Memphis, B.B.'s adopted hometown and the spiritual headwaters of the Mississippi Delta.

The Delta is a seven-thousand-square-mile alluvial plain between the Yazoo River and the Mississippi, beginning where the two waterways almost converge near Memphis, then fattening to the south until the rivers begin to draw closer once again and finally merge at Vicksburg. The soil is almost impossibly rich, owing to the sediment deposited while the two rivers periodically flooded and meandered back and forth over the millennia, like water hoses turned up high and let loose in slow motion. In fact, much of the Delta was unsuitable for permanent settlement until the nineteenth century, when its forests were cleared for timber, its rivers tamed by irrigation ditches, and levees constructed largely by black Americans, who were first transported to the region as slaves but who also settled there in large numbers after emancipation at the end of the Civil War. The Delta's small towns are connected by long sections of two-lane highway straight as pine trees and are entirely interdependent, making the whole of the Delta more like one vast city with widely spread out neighborhoods than a region with distinct municipalities. For the entire time humans have lived in the Delta, their communities and cultures have been inextricably linked to the land; sports fans at Delta State University today root unironically for their mascot, the fighting okra.

In his 1948 essay "Where I Was Born and Raised," David Cohn famously declared that the Mississippi Delta begins in the lobby of the Peabody Hotel in Memphis and ends some two hundred miles south at Catfish Row in Vicksburg. The crux of his argument is that the opulent lobby of the Peabody, where could be seen "everybody who is anybody in the Delta" and where ducks still play in a fountain at the center of an enormous room with stained glass in a ceiling more than two stories high, was the "financial, social, and cultural capital" of the region, made so by the white moneymen who struck deals and loaned and borrowed between one another to reap the fiscal harvest from the Delta's agricultural bounty. It ended down at Catfish Row in Vicksburg, where black residents got together to socialize, simply because that's where the rivers converge. "Here are no marble fountains," he wrote, "no orchestras playing at dinner, no movement of bell-boys in bright uniforms. Tumble-down shacks lean crazily over the Mississippi River far below. Inside them are dice games and 'Georgia skin'; the music of guitars, the aroma of love, and the soul-satisfying scent of catfish frying to luscious golden-brown in sizzling skillets."

Today there are no dice games at Catfish Row and no sultry blues cranking out of precariously perched shacks, just a charming little city park in a town struggling to maintain any economy at all, a sleepy shell of the southern powerhouse Vicksburg once was. And up in Memphis the Peabody is a sparkly but cloying bucket list line item for—there is simply no other way to put it—white retirees. The two endpoints still serve as good delineators of the scope of the Delta, but as to where it begins and ends Cohn had it all wrong in 1948 and wrong still today. Though the river and much of the Delta's produce flowed south, much of the money, power, and cultural capital flowed north. If at either of the two points Cohn identified, life in the Delta began at Catfish Row, on the backs of poor black people who carved the landscape out of the wilderness and farmed its fields; it ended at the Peabody, where rich white men turned cotton into cash and cash into more of itself.

The significance of the difference is that life and culture in the Mississippi Delta issue most prominently from the black people who live there. This was true in 1948, when Cohn wrote that "the Negro completely dominates the Delta in numbers" and that "the one fact indispensable to an understanding of this society" is that black residents composed more than two-thirds of the Delta's population. And it remains true today, though since 1940 the region has lost more than half its population, owing to the flight of blacks in the Great Migration, whites in the wake of integration, and both races in the face of startlingly sheer economic decline. The culture of the Delta, whether it be the blues, the food, or the hot sauce, is largely, though by no means exclusively, a product of the culture of its black residents, like Argia B. Collins Sr. before he fled north to Chicago. It is for this reason—because Africans were some of the first people on earth to come into possession of the chili, because they helped bring chilies to the United States, usually by way of the Caribbean, and because they were first enslaved and later simply poor, and thus great stewards and innovators of the people's condiment—that hot sauce has such a deeply anchored home in the Mississippi Delta.

In any event, for a journey through the Delta, Memphis is as good a place as any to start. In the city you can begin to feel the frayed and weathered cultural edges of the region. For one thing, the black population is higher than in any other sizable town in Tennessee, or in nearby Arkansas and Kentucky, for that matter. For another, the blues has an exalted place in Memphis's concept of itself, on full display while I was in town as pilgrims flocked to the B.B. King Blues Club and Grill on Beale Street to pay homage to the fallen giant. It's in the barbecue, and in the small-town spirit that envelops barbecue culture wherever it thrives, also evident while I was in town as locals and restaurateurs banded to together to keep the deeply loved family-owned barbecue joint Cozy Corner afloat in the wake of a devastating fire. And did I mention it's in the barbecue? Which can also reliably be had at lunch and well into the evening—a rarity among truly great barbecue places—at any of the three locations of the local chain Central BBQ, which has its own selection of delectable house-made sauces, including a reasonably hot one.

A key difference between Memphis and the Delta it sits atop is that Memphis is a city on the up-and-up. After decades of economic rot, Memphis's once skeletal downtown is fleshing out again. Business offices are returning, and entrepreneurs are launching new products, like the locally produced, small-batch hot sauces from Crazy Good Specialty Foods, founded in Memphis in 2010. And if Gus's World Famous Hot & Spicy Fried Chicken is any indication, Memphis's culinary traditions are alive and thriving.

The story goes like this: Long ago in the tiny town of Mason, Tennessee, about forty miles from Memphis, a man with the magnificent name of Napoleon Vanderbilt started experimenting with hot sauce and fried chicken at his small eatery that catered to black patrons. At white establishments in the segregated South, black customers, like Napoleon, had to order and collect their food at the back door. But Napoleon's fried chicken flipped the script, delightfully illustrating how we are all reduced by racism and segregation. Just as blacks couldn't eat at white restaurants, whites had to slink by the back door at Napoleon's to order his spicy fried chicken to go.

Napoleon's chicken became so loved by so many that in 1973, after the main legal buttresses of Jim Crow had been dismantled, according to the restaurant's own account white citizens put the money together to buy materials for a new building at which all would be welcome. Napoleon named the new place Maggie's Short Orders, after his wife, and business boomed for a decade until their deaths in 1983. Napoleon's son Gus inherited his dad's recipe and renamed the restaurant Gus's World Famous Hot & Spicy Fried Chicken.

Today Gus's has five locations across Tennessee, plus locations in Arkansas, Texas, Mississippi, Kansas, Illinois, Georgia, and Missouri, with reports of new locations to come. If you go to the one in downtown Memphis, get there early because even with all his new locations Gus still can't churn out his spicy fried chicken fast enough, and a rather long line tends to form outside (a line that, as I saw with my own eyes, does not disperse even in the event of a downpour).

Before I left Memphis, I texted my friend Matt Bengloff, a bona fide New York City Yankee who fell in love with the Delta and now lives in Cleveland, Mississippi, where he owns a home and frozen yogurt business called Delta Dairy (damn good ice cream sandwiches, by the way). I've been a blues fan a long time, and I was excited to be entering the heartland of that most American of all music genres. I was in search of spicy food, but there was one additional thing I hoped to find. I asked Matt if he could point me to the fabled crossroads where legendary bluesman Robert Johnson is supposed to have traded his soul to the devil in exchange for his otherworldly blues guitar chops.

"There are so many. I love it," Matt wrote back. "All the blues historians fight about it." He said I could spend a whole day just driving around to the different intersections that lay claim to the myth. So I did what any reasonable person in my situation would do and Googled it. Matt wasn't wrong.

The Mississippi Delta Tourism Association lists a total of five crossroads in or near different towns that claim to be the one of legend (plus three separate towns that lay claim to Johnson's burial site). The five intersections are in Cleveland, Tunica, Greenwood, Clarksdale, and Rosedale, the last two being the most often mentioned. Clarksdale's claim seems based primarily on the town's indisputably important place in blues history and the ostentatious and singularly unbluesy sign that demarcates the supposed spot. So I skipped it. Instead, from Memphis I drove south on Route 61 through Tunica and Clarksdale to Rosedale, a tiny town right by the Mississippi River in the heart of the Delta.

I parked my car near the intersection of Routes 1 and 8 on the outskirts of town and walked to the crossroads. With the caveat that I do not, on principle, believe in the devil and, more important, that were I to encounter the devil, I would have been in no way prepared to sell him my soul in exchange for any skills, guitar-related or otherwise, I waited to see if he'd appear. It was quiet. Now and then people drove by waving, smiling, and laughing. They knew exactly what I was up to.

Rosedale's claim to the infamous intersection stems in part from the lyrics of Johnson's "Traveling Riverside Blues" ("Lord, I'm goin' to Rosedale, gon' take my rider by my side"), as well as from the testimony of bluesman Son House, one of the few sources close to the action who has been quoted asserting that Johnson "sold his soul to the devil to get to play like that," and who claimed to know for certain that Johnson did the deed at Routes 1 and 8. In addition, according to the now defunct Crossroads Blues Society based in Rosedale, a bluesman named Henry Goodman claimed to have had a vision in which he saw what Johnson had done. A transcript of Goodman's account was obtained by the Crossroads Blues Society. In the vision, Goodman saw Johnson encounter a figure, the devil, at the intersection. The devil had a howling dog at his side and told Johnson that he could turn east on Route 8 toward Cleveland or head south on Route 1 back to Beulah, but if he meant to go to Rosedale, then he'd be making a pact with the Prince of Darkness. "My left hand will be forever wrapped around your soul, and your music will possess all who hear it," the devil is supposed to have said. Johnson thought it over. "Step back, Devil-Man," he said. "I'm going to Rosedale. I am the Blues."

So the devil moved aside. "Go on, Robert Johnson," he said. "You the King of the Delta Blues. Go on home to Rosedale. And when you get on up in town, you get you a plate of hot tamales because you going to be needing something on your stomach where you're headed."

I suppose it's no secret why Rosedale's claim is my favorite.

The Mississippi Delta hot tamale is a delicious gustatory tradition as shrouded in mystery as Johnson's supernatural contract. Usually served with hot sauce and made of cornmeal and spicy beef, pork, or even chicken or turkey, the Delta hot tamale is basically the same as any tamale one might find south of the border. Historians dispute how the hot tamale came to be a Delta staple. Some say American soldiers brought the tamale tradition back from the Mexican-American War; others say the hot tamale has always been in the Delta as a food traditionally eaten by indigenous people in the area, but most people seem to agree that Mexican migrant workers in the Delta introduced hot tamales.

Wherever they came from, it's obvious why hot tamales caught on in the Delta: in addition to being inexpensive to make and calorie dense, their capsaicin content would have been all too familiar to the people there, especially the ones of African descent.

Blanche Turnage was born and raised in Rosedale and still lives there today.

"My earliest memory of hot tamales is when my family would make them and sell them when I was a girl," she told me. I asked her if hot tamales are always by definition spicy. It may seem a stupid question, but I wanted to clarify that the *hot* in *hot tamales* was in reference to chilies, not temperature.

"Oh yeah, they are," she said. "I never even put hot sauce on hot tamales. If you just use enough pepper, that does it every time."

Today you can get great hot tamales throughout the Delta; in Rosedale at the White Front Cafe or TJ's Wild Wings & Things (the latter store's name underlines a chicken wing–related point I've made previously and will spare the reader repeating). The Gin Mill Gallery restaurant adjacent the B.B. King Museum in Indianola does a fantastic tamale. My favorite hot tamales were had at Solly's in Vicksburg, where a recipe nearly a century old is still being prepared with love four generations on, though the original Henry "Papa" Solly—who, for what it's worth, said he learned to make hot tamales in California—long ago passed away.

Delta tamales tend to be served with all kinds of hot sauces. The White Front Cafe offers its tasty tamales with a depressingly boring, generic hot sauce packet (something like Taco Bell's hot sauce). Solly's serves its tamales with Cajun Chef hot sauce. Most often you'll find tamales, like every other savory meal in the Delta, served at a table with Louisiana hot sauce, the hands-down regional favorite, and possibly with a bottle of clear, spicy vinegar with chilies soaking in it, a homemade concoction folks in the Delta tend to call "pepper sauce."

After waiting around for some time at the crossroads in Rosedale, getting laughs and encouraging thumbs-up from passersby, I finally gave up on the devil. I returned to the car, pulled out my phone, and called Eustace Harold Winn IV, who is something of an angel to all who know him and lives in a town not far down the road.

The interrobang is a little-used punctuation mark (I promise I'm going somewhere with this—stick with me) designed to exclaim a question. Usually in informal English prose we represent this idea with an exclamation point followed by a question mark (like so: !?), but in its perfect oneness the interrobang, to me, flawlessly expresses the surprise, the sudden, delighted excitement, and the sincerity implicit in the statement it punctuates. Most of us exchange rote pleasantries like "how are you?" multiple times a day without even reflecting on what we're saying, but we generally don't shout such questions, nor do we ask them with delighted surprise. This is all to explain why I will now violate mainstream grammatical convention and deploy an interrobang, in an effort to more perfectly portray Eustace. I'd met him at Matt Bengloff's wedding years earlier, and we hadn't spoken since. He had no warning I'd be calling.

"Hi, Eustace? This is Denver Ni—"

"Hey, Denver! How you doin' man?"

Eustace is tall, gregarious, and something of a living legend, seemingly on a first-name basis with the entire Mississippi Delta. His open-heartedness reflects the rich, homespun goodness still present in the Delta. "Come on to Benoit!" he said. "Meet me at the gas station."

Eustace grew up in Greenville, Mississippi, and farms about seven hundred acres—sometimes more depending on what fields he's renting—near the tiny town of Benoit. He lives at Hollywood

Plantation, so named because of an abundance of holly trees on the land, and is caretaker of a regal old plantation house on the property recently rescued from ruin and lovingly restored. The house was constructed by Eustace's ancestor Judge J. C. Burrus and completed just before the outbreak of the Civil War; it's thought to have been spared being torched by Union troops simply because the Yankees liked and respected Judge Burrus, perhaps because a former classmate of his at the University of Virginia was in command of Union forces in the area. It's the only antebellum house in Bolivar County. Today it's known as the Baby Doll House, having been used as the set of the 1956 blockbuster film *Baby Doll*, a scandalous movie in its time coproduced by Elia Kazan and Tennessee Williams. The film won Kazan a Golden Globe award for best director, despite (or because of) attempts to censor it for its highly sexualized content; the movie is credited with popularizing the baby doll nightgown.

I left my car at the gas station and jumped into Eustace's truck. We drove south out of town to go fishing, but as we neared the lake, an army of rain clouds formed over the horizon and a foreboding drizzle quickly became a downpour. We doubled back to Eustace's place at Hollywood Plantation, cracked open a couple of beers, and stood on the porch to watch the sky drench the fields.

"Isn't this fun? Denver's adventures in the Delta," Eustace remarked. "We didn't go fishing, but we had an adventure. Old B.B. sent the rain down to the dry Delta this weekend, I'm telling you. He wanted us farmers to do good. I mean it has been *dumping*." He was quiet for a minute, and we let the sound of rain on the roof fill the silence with eyes locked on the wet earth. Then Eustace turned to me and grinned, hugely. "Hanging out in a place where things are growing because it's raining—it makes you feel good!"

Eustace's earliest recollection of hot sauce is one of those all-too-common traumatic memories. A little kid on a church trip—his parents were chaperoning, so he came along even though he was a lot younger than the others on the trip—he was asleep on the bus when the older kids doused his lips in hot sauce. He woke up screaming bloody murder. His mom was furious at the older kids, etcetera. Eustace said it seems just about everyone in the Delta likes hot sauce, but he didn't eat it for years after that.

"I finally started putting it on my deer meat, with the ketchup. Then I started putting it on my fish. I like Louisiana hot sauce and Tabasco on fried fish," he said. "And then there's the Grazi sauce. I've always known about that."

I'd never heard the word before—*Grazi* (rhymes with Ozzy). It would turn out to be one of the more unique sauces I've encountered, a dark, thick, and creamy sauce, with exotic tones of cinnamon, mildly spicy but not unnoticeably so, and significantly different from both the Louisiana hot sauce and the homemade spicy vinegar pepper sauces so common throughout the Delta. And thanks to the story behind it, Grazi sauce is a delicious reminder that while the Mississippi Delta may be a region steeped in black history and a vital center for African American culture, like the rest of America it's also a melting pot. Yes, it's the blues. But it's also jazz. Which is a nice thought, since as I would come to learn, Grazi hasn't always rhymed with Ozzy—the way Miss Grazi pronounced her own name rhymes with *jazzy*.

When she was eighteen years old, a young woman named Antonia moved from Alessandria in northern Italy to Rosedale, Mississippi, where she married fellow Italian immigrant Augusto Graziosi. Together they operated a farm off Route 1 just south of town (not far from the famed intersection) until Augusto's death in 1940. At under five feet tall, Graziosi, or "Miss Grazi," as people tended to call her, was described as a "dynamo" by her grandson, the now-deceased Delta journalist Leroy Morganti, in a charming remembrance written about his grandmother for the small journal *USA Deep South*. She continued to run the farm by herself for the rest of her life, keeping milk cows and chickens and raising enough vegetables to sell at the local grocery store. A row of three white pet ducks followed her around the farm morning to night. She liked to finish the day with a thumb or two of bourbon. She also grew the chilies she used in the concoction that came eventually to be called Miz Grazi's Hot Stuff, known colloquially today as Grazi sauce.

It can be hard to find Grazi sauce these days. Miss Grazi has long since left us, and the sauce is now prepared and bottled by the Louisiana-based hot sauce company Panola. It's rumored to be available for retail sale sometimes at various locations—at the grocery store in Rosedale, for example, though when I went, floor clerks hadn't a clue what I was talking about—but the place Grazi sauce can most reliably be found is Backyard Burgers, a regional burger chain founded by the family in Cleveland, Mississippi, where you can order a good-for-fast-food burger with Grazi sauce dripping from between the buns or on the side. If they've enough on hand, they'll sometimes even sell you a bottle.

The hot sauce scene in Mississippi today is about as lively as anything can be in that deepest reach of the sultry Deep South. At the Delta Meat Market in Cleveland you can usually find a nameless pureed hot sauce made by the vat that is leaps and bounds hotter than most hot sauces in the area. Mississippi Comeback Sauce, a kind of rémoulade with the tiniest bit of a kick, is still a statewide favorite used as a salad dressing, as a sandwich spread, or as a dipping sauce for fried everything. In 2014 downriver from Vicksburg, in Natchez, the oldest permanent European settlement on the Mississippi River, the Aldridge family launched a line of small-batch hot sauces under the name D'Evereux Foods. (Like some other companies in the region they call them pepper sauces but, you know, "tomato tomahto.") The company name pays homage to D'Evereux, the appellation given the antebellum plantation home with an iconic red roof where family patriarch Courtney Aldridge first concocted the recipe. If D'Evereux Foods' early efforts are any indication, Mississippi's hot sauce tradition is in good hands.

This living tradition came to Mississippi with its immigrants, like the Italian teenager and her cinnamon hot sauce, Mexican migrants and their hot tamales, and the many descendants of enslaved Africans, who tamed the wilderness, spiced up their humble cuisine, and invented the blues. Like the blues, it's a tradition created and introduced to the United States by people all too familiar with struggle, with suffering, with pain. And like the blues, it's a tradition that followed the original great American highway, the Mississippi River, to the industrial northern cities like Chicago, Washington, DC, and Buffalo. And its roots go deeper still.

The word *mambo*, which other than lots of sugar seems to be about the only commonality—slight spelling variations notwithstanding—among the different sauces that share the moniker, is also the word in Haitian Vodou for a female priestess, like Rose, who introduced Baron Ambrosia to her religion and its spicy spiritual cuisine. One has nothing to lean on but conjecture, that ricketiest of foundations, but one still guesses that a linguistic lineage back to Africa is buried deep within mambo sauce DNA.

Also, in Vodou, crossroads have a special significance as a portal between worlds. They are particularly important for Baron Samedi, who, as the Loa responsible for shepherding souls between the lands of the living and the dead, is the guardian of the crossroads. Like other aspects of ancient African culture, the symbolism of the crossroads echoes through African American folklore and in the blues fables we still tell each other today. Robert Johnson didn't just sell his soul to the devil—he sold it to the most hot sauce–loving Loa of all.

9

ÇA PIQUE

It is a city of pimps, prostitutes, and gamblers; French-speaking grandes dames who wear the eighteenth century in their black lace shawls; hoodoo-working Negroes; oyster-fishing Jugoslavians; industrious Germans; fiesta-loving Italians; Spaniards, Greeks, Jews, Filipinos, Chinese; and, on the extreme periphery, a large group of Anglo-Saxons who sometimes look strangely out of place in this least typically American of American cities.
—DAVID L. COHN, 1940

I stepped off the New York subway and onto the street not far from Pratt Institute and the Brooklyn Navy Yard, through an exceedingly nondescript doorway and into the Corridor Gallery, where an art installation was on display called *Hot Sauce and Brown Liquor*. Along the walls were pieces by various artists united, unsurprisingly, by hot sauce and brown liquor themes: paintings of human organs done in Sriracha, a marble sculpture of a bottle of Johnny Walker Black Label, the capsaicin molecule as glowing neon pink signage.

A group of striking prints hanging on the walls featured pop icons, from Marilyn Monroe to Quentin Tarantino to Boris Karloff's Frankenstein, all in black and white and pouring, caressing, or otherwise getting soaked in bright red hot sauce. Usually the work featured a bottle of Tabasco somewhere. Except it wasn't Tabasco. A closer look at the label and I could see clearly it read TOBASCO. And in the space where a bottle of Tabasco has McILHENNY CO. this bottle had MAUNSEL WHITE on it. Where a normal bottle has the name of the Tabasco headquarters, AVERY ISLAND, LA, this had THIEVERY ISLAND, LA. And below that, where a bottle of Tabasco notes EST. 1868, this included ORIGINAL SINCE 1858.

Weird.

I found a document online that accompanied the series titled *The Hot Sauce Manifesto*. It's a fitting preamble for what came next. It begins thusly:

"What you are about to absorb is as truthful as anything that can be absorbed in this time we live in. While some of it exists as opinion—the vast majority of it resonates with the facts it is taken from. What lies ahead is a serpentine trail of thought, theory, conjecture, convolution, and conspiracy . . . And—like most serpentine trails—it eventually leads down the rabbit hole."

Fortunately I'd arranged to meet the artist, David Taylor, or just Vid for short, who agreed to accompany me on my journey down this particular rabbit hole. We met at a bar near the gallery, grabbed a couple of drinks, and huddled in a corner to sort out just what in the hell this was all about. He started with the beginning of his hot sauce obsession.

By day, Vid is the production director for jazz at Lincoln Center, where he works with big crews of unionized stagehands. Meals are provided for crew members, and at one event the caterer brought a large bucket of tiny Tabasco bottles. Many went unused, so Vid took them home and turned them into a small shadow box frame around a painting of Marilyn Monroe. So began his hot sauce project.

The project, as the manifesto says, "is an exploration of Toxic Consumption in our modern era. It's about the pervasiveness of pop culture across all boundaries. It's about corporate greed and its use of mass media to justify mass production with a reliance on mass consumption. It's about consumers buying into their own oppression. It's about pop art and its use of appropriation."

Vid Taylor's hot sauce project is vast in both scope and depth, drawing conspiratorial connections between the illusory nature of the capsaicin-pain effect, the insidious and corrosive effects of pop culture on our brains and modern society, and the nature of appropriation in mass media, as in pop art. As he delved deeper into the project, he discovered a conspiracy theory of sorts about the origins of Tabasco that mirrors the theory of appropriation at the center of his art. The story, as recounted by Vid Taylor based on his research and that of writer Chuck Evans, goes like this.

In about 1796, a thirteen-year-old orphan boy from Limerick, Ireland, arrived in North America. His name was Maunsel White. Little is known about his early life, but at some point he took up residence in southern Louisiana, which became part of the United States with Thomas Jefferson's Louisiana Purchase in 1803. White lived in Plaquemines Parish, the sliver of lowland and bayou country that tracks the Mississippi as it winds southeasterly out of New Orleans and finally to its terminus at the Gulf of Mexico.

As the War of 1812 neared its end, White was placed in charge of a regiment of Louisiana militia, for which he served as colonel alongside a Baton Rouge physician named Dudley Avery. At the conclusion of the war, Colonel White got involved in several mercantile pursuits, financing the construction of a canal in New Orleans and raising sugarcane, corn, and other crops at his Deer Range Plantation. He also served on a state commission to oversee the construction of the new state capitol building in Baton Rouge, along with attorney and fellow commissioner Daniel Dudley Avery, son of the physician White had served with in the war.

In 1847, White attended a reception in New Orleans to celebrate veterans returning from the Mexican-American War. The soldiers had arrived by way of the Mexican port city of Veracruz, near the region of Mexico that today contains the state named Tabasco.

Not long after the reception, White began cultivating chilies he called tobasco peppers, which he had presumably received from a soldier returning from the war, who may have brought them home out of horticultural curiosity.

Here's a local newspaper article from January 26, 1850, describing White's new pursuit: "Col. White has introduced the celebrated tobasco red pepper, the very strongest of all peppers, of which he cultivated a large quantity with the view of supplying his neighbors, and diffusing it throughout the state." The article goes on to discuss White's recipe for preparing a sauce from the chilies.

"Owing to its oleaginous character, Col. White found it impossible to preserve it by drying; but by pouring strong vinegar on it after boiling, he has made a sauce or pepper decoction of it, which possesses in a most concentrated form all the quantities of the vegetable. A single drop of the sauce will flavor a whole plate of soup or other food. The use of a decoction like this, particularly in preparing the food for laboring persons, would be exceedingly beneficial in a relaxing climate like this."

In 1859, according to Vid Taylor, Maunsel White started selling his Tobasco Sauce commercially.

While Col. White was cooking up his spicy sauce and slinging the results, a wealthy, self-made millionaire banker with a reputation as a libertine named Edmund McIlhenny—he's described in his company's authorized history as a "bon vivant"—was spending his days racing his boat named *The Secret*, riding a flashy mare named

Fashion, and generally raising hell on the streets of New Orleans. McIlhenny was an eligible bachelor if ever there was one, but he had a dark secret—hence the name of the boat, according to company history: he was in love with his best friend's daughter. Her name was Mary Eliza Avery. Her father was Daniel Dudley Avery, who had served on the commission to oversee the construction of the state capitol along with Colonel Maunsel White.

Daniel Dudley Avery had married into ownership of a sugar plantation on a salt dome that rose out of Bayou Petite Anse several miles south of New Iberia in the heart of Cajun country, which eventually came to be called Avery Island. When the young woman turned twenty, McIlhenny asked Avery for his blessing, which he did not at first grant to his hell-raising pal (because who would?). Eventually he relented, and the two were married in 1859.

Less than a year later, the outbreak of the Civil War drove the young family to seek refuge at Avery Island. Around the same time, the family discovered that the island in the bayou was in fact a giant dome of salt—eons ago the region had been a seabed, a small part of which had been driven upward by geologic forces, creating the bulge of salt in the surrounding swamp. That discovery made the island invaluable as a source of salt for the Confederacy, as well as for the Union once federal troops captured it during the war and drove the Averys into exile in Texas.

The Civil War brought ruin to the plantation at Avery Island. After the war, McIlhenny returned to New Orleans in search of work to repair his finances, only to find that a washed-up, middle-aged former party animal was not employable in the military-occupied southern port city. He returned to Avery Island and, like many a retiree before and after him, set his mind to gardening.

Family lore is unclear as to why McIlhenny started making hot sauce or even how exactly he got the chilies, but, according to the authorized family history, it is generally agreed that he got them in New Orleans from an American soldier who had recently returned to the United States from travels in Mexico. McIlhenny first made a pepper sauce for the family table and later, packaged in used cologne bottles, for family and friends. The stuff caught on, so he bought a whole bunch of new cologne bottles, increased production, and the rest, as it so often is, is history.

Vid Taylor contends that Maunsel White and Edmund McIlhenny, both being high-society types in antebellum New Orleans, when the population of the city was just north of one hundred thousand, very likely knew each other. Since White made his Tobasco sauce well before McIlhenny made his Tabasco sauce, and owing to the other linkages between White and the Avery family, Taylor surmises that McIlhenny got his chilies from White, who died during the Civil War and wouldn't have been around to set the record straight when Tabasco hit the shelves. White's family continued selling his hot sauce for a couple of decades thereafter— the 1875 Christmas dinner menu for the Arlington Hotel in Hot Springs, Arkansas, includes a tantalizing mention under "Relishes" of "Tobasco Red Pepper Sauce," though it's impossible to know if that's a reference to White's sauce or an instance of a creative spelling, which was not uncommon in the age before mass media. In any event, White's Tobasco sauce hasn't been sold commercially for more than a century. Something called Maunsel White's 1812 Wine Sauce is available at a few shops in New Orleans, but be warned that it is not in any discernible sense a hot sauce. A small paragraph on the bottle repeats the claim that Maunsel White was the originator of Tabasco sauce while clarifying that 1812 Wine Sauce is unrelated to that original concoction.

The Hot Sauce Manifesto is, at its essence, not a work of history but an artist statement for a series that critiques the toxicity and fundamentally derivative nature of pop culture. Being the most popular hot sauce on earth, Tabasco makes for a good villain, and the Maunsel White historical angle—in which McIlhenny uses White's creation without attribution—parallels the way pop culture cannibalizes itself, rehashing the same tunes, themes, and stories rather than creating new ones. The art is beautiful and impactful. As to whether or not Edmund McIlhenny really did take anything from Maunsel White in any untoward way, there's no way to know for certain. The timeline is such that it does seem likely White gave the peppers to McIlhenny. On the other hand, it seems just as likely that if he did, White would have been thrilled to see his acquaintance making a go of it with the exotic Mexican chilies. It seems just as likely that McIlhenny was at the same Mexican-American War veterans' celebration where Maunsel White apparently got his chilies. Most of all, except for as a historical curiosity and as the premise for an artistic cultural critique, the controversy all seems rather irrelevant.

The McIlhenny Company doesn't think so. A section on the company website is dedicated to debunking "myths" surrounding the origin of Tabasco, namely that Maunsel White had anything to do with it.

On a visit to Avery Island I met with Tony Simmons, the great-great-grandson of Edmund McIlhenny and CEO of the McIlhenny Company. He was kind enough to grant me an interview despite the fact that when we shook hands, I was red faced and sweating rather profusely after making the mistake of taking a bite of a fresh tabasco pepper right off the plant growing outside his office. I asked Simmons about the Maunsel White theory.

"When you only have three ingredients . . . You look at the bottle and there's red tabasco pepper mash, vinegar, and a little bit of salt. I mean, it's kind of hard to have a secret recipe," he said. "And we don't cook it."

This is indeed a key difference between whatever Maunsel White made and the process employed to make the Tabasco enjoyed by so many today.

The McIlhenny Company puts about twenty acres in tabasco peppers on Avery Island. Direct descendants, it is said, of Edmund's original crop, those plants are allowed to go to seed, and the harvested seeds are sent to farms in Guatemala, Honduras, Nicaragua, Panama, Colombia, Peru, Ecuador, Zambia, Zimbabwe, Swaziland, and Mozambique, where the peppers are raised, harvested, and mashed on site. Salt mined at Avery Island is shipped to the farms, where it is added to the mash, which is then shipped back to Avery Island to be transferred to retired oak bourbon barrels to age for up to three years. When the time is right—Simmons's son, who oversees this part of the process, tastes the mash at least once a day—the mash is moved into bigger barrels, where vinegar is stirred in for about a month. That brew is strained, bottled, and shipped to stores around the world, where it is purchased and taken home to the kitchen pantries of hot sauce lovers like my dad. And quite a few other people too.

The McIlhenny Company employs about two hundred people, many of whom live in company-owned rental houses on Avery Island. Simmons told me he has, at last count, 336 cousins, but the family-owned company has only about 130 shareholders and only three or four family members are active employees at any given time. An unspecified number of family members and associates are said to live on the island in houses that, along with spooky old abandoned homes, dot the labyrinthine roads that run throughout the property—on my visit to the McIlhenny Company office I missed a turn and after realizing my mistake made the most of it by playing the dumb reporter, meandering through oak forest and Spanish moss for as far as my then-new fear of ghosts (more on that later) would allow.

It's easy to see why someone would want to live on Avery Island. The place is idyllic. In addition to the obvious amenities of country living, residents can, if they wish, enjoy the fact that the island is something of a bird sanctuary. It also features the 170-acre Jungle Gardens, a gorgeous spread of walking paths through giant gnarled oak groves, flower gardens, and swamp home to alligators. Rounding out the beauty of the place is a Chinese-themed garden where sits a reportedly nine-hundred-year-old statue of Buddha—in the 1920s a Chinese warlord is said to have sent the statue to New York for unknown reasons, where it sat in a warehouse, unclaimed, until, in what looks to me like one of the better practical gags ever pulled, two of then-CEO Ned McIlhenny's friends bought it for him and shipped it to Avery Island as a surprise.

The presence of Avery Island might alone be enough to make southern Louisiana America's hot sauce heartland—it's hard to miss echoes of the Cora creation myth in the twin pillars of salt and chili— but hard numbers seal the deal. More than a fifth of all people employed in the hot sauce industry in the United States work in Louisiana, more than California (17 percent), more than Texas (10 percent), more than Arizona (6 percent), more than New Mexico (1 percent), or anywhere else. That includes the makers of Tabasco; Crystal in New Orleans; Louisiana Brand hot sauce and Trappey's, both in New Iberia; and Panola out of Lake Providence in the northeastern corner of the state. And there are also smaller name sauces, like Evangeline and Cajun Chef, made by the same company out of charming St. Martinville.

At the Louisiana Hot Sauce Expo in Lafayette I was standing at the CaJohn booth trying a surprisingly good hot sauce–infused lemonade when I overheard a man next to me.

"*Comment ça va?*" he asked the guy manning the booth.

These days it's not terribly common to hear people speaking French in public in southern Louisiana. Many French-speaking adults grew up speaking to monolinguistic grandparents or in bilingual homes, but young people today tend to learn French in school, and the language is more a cultural artifact and a mark of ethnic pride than a living language in common usage.

Curious, I wheeled around immediately to find Wilford Bouton, age sixty-two, a barrel-chested Lafayette native with a goatee and a ready smile.

"I love hot food," Bouton said when I asked what brought him to the hot sauce expo. "I had surgery on my neck, and it's hard to eat hot food when you had surgery on your neck, but it's too good to let go. It makes you happy. It makes you enjoy your food," he said, tacking on the truism long known to many a dieter and chilihead alike. "The spicier it is the less you eat—*c'est bon.*"

One is given to wonder why Cajun people took so fiercely to spicy food. They are, after all, ethnically French—a culture with a rich and multifarious cuisine, to be sure, but not exactly one known for its use of chilies. I venture to guess that the Cajun affinity for chilies has to do more with their status long ago as among the lowest of the low on the American hierarchy.

The original Cajuns were French Canadian colonists exiled from what they called Acadie in and around Nova Scotia, after the English forcibly deported them beginning in 1755 in concert with the outbreak of the French and Indian War (or the Seven Years War, if you're reading this outside the United States). Homeless and destitute, they made their way to other French possessions in the New World. In the end, many landed in the Spanish-occupied formerly French colony of Louisiana, where they were welcome to eke out a living in the alligator- and mosquito-infested swampland if they dared. They introduced themselves to their new neighbors as Acadienne—say the word out loud to yourself in your best French accent and you'll see how the term *Cajun* came to be.

In southern Louisiana their long journey in search of a home was over, and Cajun people flourished. They built towns, hunted and fished in the woods and swamps, and became familiar with the decidedly non-Canadian flora and fauna of their new homeland. One can imagine the odd looks given the first Cajun to come waltzing back to camp with a dead alligator slung over his shoulder. And for all the reasons poor people have always loved chilies—because they're cheap, flavorful, hearty, and filling—they learned to love spicy food.

I confess to having a strong affinity for southern Louisiana. Dark roux chicken and sausage gumbo is, hands down, my single favorite food on God's green earth—when I've got a batch on hand, I spend several days in a state of delighted uncomfortable fullness until it is gone. I am charmed by the way people from that part of the world wish each other a happy Mardi Gras the way the rest of us wish each other a merry Christmas as the holiday approaches, still weeks away. There is a pervasive spirit of joie de vivre at work in the low country from roughly Ville Platte south to the Gulf of Mexico and between Lake Charles in the east and New Orleans in the west. It's the kind of heritable lust for life that can only come from extended pain and hardship. When life teaches you, repeatedly, that to live is to suffer, you learn to live for what pleasure you can, and you teach your children to do the same. And in this life, when tragedy can strike at any moment, there is simply no time for bland food. You cook like you live: richly. And you cook with chilies—because you can afford them, because they're tasty, and, as Wilford said, because they make you happy.

Like people in many cultures, Cajuns tell stories of ghosts and the like. In one common tale, recounted by Richard Schweid in his wonderful 1989 book *Hot Peppers: The Story of Cajuns and Capsi-cum*, a certain witch was believed to take off her skin at night and go around riding people while they slept. (Waking with dirty feet and toenails was the telltale sign you'd been ridden by a witch.) One evening, an enterprising witch hunter found the witch's empty epidermis and sprinkled chili powder in it. When the witch went to put her birthday suit back on in the morning, she leaped in pain as her own skin seemed to be rejecting her. "Skinny, don't you know me? What's the matter skin? Don't you know me, my old skin?" she cried, hopping up and down in pain. When the townspeople saw her jumping up and down, they knew they had their mark and put her to death.

Officially, I do not believe in ghosts, but this part of the world has a way of sinking into you, like the earth itself seems to be forever sinking into the bayou.

I spent a weekend running around Cajun country with a group of friends: the notorious itinerant Aric S. Queen, plus a New Orleans–based artist and two roadies on a short vacation from rock 'n' roller Marilyn Manson's Hell Not Hallelujah Tour (a tour, strangely enough, that Manson said was partly inspired by the culture of southern Louisiana).

We stopped for a beer at a nondescript bar in St. Martinville, one of the oldest towns in the region, where the signs are still in French and a charming square surrounds the Catholic church at the very center of town. As we walked outside, I noticed a small shack across the street—the kind either that could have been abandoned and left to rot for fifty years or that serves amazing BBQ. I read the sign: Mr. Francis. Home of original hot links!

I walked across the street and peered in the open window. I saw no one but hollered, "Did y'all really invent the hot link?"

Like a puppet from beneath a stage, a tiny woman emerged from under the window in front of me. She grinned wildly and almost whispered in a rasp, "Fo' fifty."

It was an amazing hot link. I was so taken with the snack and everything about the moment that unless by the time you are reading this I have lost an appendage, I have "$4.50" tattooed on my arm. I left the shack and walked to the town square to deliver a bite I saved for Aric.

We spent a few minutes relaxing in front of the church. There was a wedding reception under way in an event space off the square, and muffled hip-hop played into the dusk. We crossed the street and got a table at Kajun King for oysters and excellent dark roux gumbo. As the sun went down, we walked kitty-corner to an old building with a wraparound second-story balcony. The sign said LA MAISON, and there was a bar inside that looked open despite being empty. We ducked in for a nightcap.

The place was deserted. We took seats at a long alligator-skin bar and ordered Sazeracs. Two perfectly nice but somehow emphatically unenthusiastic teenagers were running the place. We asked if we could see the upstairs, and one of them said sure, whatever, if we wanted, but it was just about dark outside and it's haunted up there. Supposedly a six-year-old girl had fallen from the balcony and was trampled to death by a team of horses. The five of us climbed the stairs and took seats on the porch, sipping cocktails, smoking cigarettes, and trying to feel the presence of the dead child. Everyone else professed to feel something, or hear something, but I felt nothing.

After a while two of our party returned to the bar downstairs while three of us sat quietly on the porch. I don't usually go in for this sort of thing, but if I'm anything, I'm willing to play along. So I spent some more time walking alone through the empty second floor, willing the ghost to communicate with me. I even spoke to her.

Nothing. Having scoured it for any sign of life or afterlife, I finally left the empty interior and returned to the balcony. I sat with my quiet disappointment for a silent moment. Then, directly behind us, a door *creaked open and slammed shut.*

We three leaped out of our chairs in unison and ran downstairs. Everyone—every single person in the building—was relaxing at the bar. I stood staring blankly for a moment and mumbled out an order for another drink, my neck hair standing on end, so visibly rattled that the bartender asked if I was OK.

"Here," she said, handing me a bottle of La Maison's own hot sauce. "On the house."

We finished our drinks and walked back to the car solemnly. Among us there was the bloated quiet of skeptics who, having played along irreverently with a ghost story, could not hide from the discomfiting fact that even if for just a moment we'd entertained the possibility that we had been in the presence of the supernatural.

Aric looked at me gravely.

"Don't ever open that bottle."

New Orleans is the only major city in America where it's still indisputably safe in any given context for a man to wear a hat. It's dirty, dangerous, barely functional, and oozing with sweaty, sexy charm. It's older than America, the birthplace of jazz and the Sazerac, and the cradle of a cuisine so rich and delectable that any time spent in the Crescent City promises to test even the most fastidiously monitored waistline—as my New Orleanian friend Dianna put it to me once, "Honey, ya gonna get fat. They put butter in the water." New Orleans is a feast in endless motion and a libertine's paradise. Fittingly, the city gets its name from the famously libidinous Philippe

II, duc d'Orléans, regent of France from 1715 to 1723, a musician, composer of operas, and foodie who threw lavish shut-in dinner parties rumored to be dens of the most lecherous vice.

In her memoir on post–Hurricane Katrina, Cheryl Wagner writes that New Orleans "has evolved into the place where Southerners send their laidback people who can't or won't get with the program—their artists, gay relatives, eternal optimists, funny hat wearers, weirdoes and intellectuals."

This charming portrait is right on but incomplete. You're unlikely to ever hear locals call the city the Big Easy, but you might hear them remark that living there ain't easy. New Orleans seethes under the weight of deep generational poverty, and it remains starkly segregated on racial lines. The city isn't as corrupt as it once was, but in a head-to-head contest for least scruples New Orleans would still trounce most American cities. Many of the streets are little more than trails of overlapping potholes. And New Orleans is steeped in violence, from the high crime rates of the late twentieth and the early twenty-first centuries all the way back to the unique part it played in America's original sin: slavery. By about 1840, New Orleans was home to America's largest slave market.

The city's important role in the development of slavery in North America is a result of its geography—at the mouth of America's first and still most important interstate highway, the Mississippi River, and a port city with longstanding economic and cultural ties to the Caribbean rim and beyond. In the eighteenth century, the corporation responsible for developing and populating France's vast New World holdings controlled a mercantile network of almost unimaginable scale extending from West Africa, whence slaves were exported, to Saint Domingue, the totalitarian nightmare later renamed Haiti after the slaves overthrew the masters, to Louisiana, and from France to Canada, down the St. Lawrence River and via a combination of overland and water routes, to the Great Lakes and down the Mississippi to the Gulf of Mexico.

Enslaved Africans appeared in Louisiana almost as soon as Europeans began moving to the area in earnest early in the eighteenth century. Owing to the fact that people of African ancestry in Louisiana were for long stretches of time governed by the French *Code Noir* and Spanish slave laws, which granted more rights to black people than they enjoyed under British and later American law, race in New Orleans meant something rather different than in the rest of the United States. New Orleans was home to a large population of free people of color when that category barely existed in most of the American South. And New Orleans's society included people of mixed-race ancestry who occupied a rung on the social ladder that simply didn't exist in the mainstream American caste system. This greater degree of freedom contributed to the development of the distinctly rich Afro-Louisianan culture of New Orleans—the culture of Mardi Gras Indians, second lines, and of Afro-Caribbean beats at Congo Square that eventually begat jazz.

Enslaved people weren't the only downtrodden inhabitants to populate France's nascent city of La Nouvelle-Orléans. Here's how Ned Sublette describes the peopling of Louisiana in his epic history *The World That Made New Orleans: From Spanish Silver to Congo Square*.

"Prostitutes and female criminals (with the fleur-de-lis branded on their shoulders to mark them as under sentence for life) were rounded up for exile to Louisiana . . . [along with] tobacco smugglers, thieves, beggars, vagabonds, orphans, the unemployed, the incorrigible, the vicious, the depraved, the wrongly accused, and bystanders. . . . To say 'Louisiana' in the France of 1719 was more or less the equivalent of saying 'Siberia' in twentieth-century Russia. Forcibly wedded prisoner couples were marched across France through town after town on their way to the port, in a rolling caravan that served as a reminder that only the dregs of society went to Louisiana, and only in chains."

Add additional waves of immigration from Spain, Ireland, Italy, Germany, Sicily, the Philippines, Vietnam, China, and many more, plus vital economic and cultural linkages to the Mississippi watershed in North America and to cities around the Caribbean (especially Havana, until the mid twentieth century), and a picture of America's sweltering Frankencity begins to take shape. As America's indisputable financial capital, New York City has its charms, but New Orleans is the real capital of the American mélange.

Poverty. The Caribbean. Proximity to Latin America. Africans. A head-spinning blend of cultures celebrating life in the face of adversity. It should be easy by now to see why hot sauce has such a firmly entrenched place in New Orleans. As my friend Sally put it to me after telling a story about learning that her favorite green chili hot sauce was being discontinued and going to "every grocery store between here, Abbeville, Lafayette, and Baton Rouge" in search of remaining bottles, "Spice is life. Salt is life. Hot sauce is life." I even met a Chihuahua in New Orleans named Chang who likes hot sauce, which threatens to undermine some very high-minded pronouncements about humanity and hot sauce made earlier in this tome. The stuff is everywhere. When one endeavors to tell one's friends one is writing a book about hot sauce, one tends to get a lot of sideways glances, but nowhere more so than in New Orleans. When I told my aforementioned friend Dianna about the project, her response was a scrunched nose followed by two words delivered with bottomless incredulity: "*Hot sauce?*" It was as if I'd suggested writing about something as banal and commonplace as the air.

Classic New Orleans cuisine belongs to a group of traditions that exist under the amorphous designation Creole. Broadly speaking, the word came into existence to differentiate people of whatever race born in the Americas rather than in the Old World (with the exception of Native Americans). Creole cuisine thus includes a tangled array of influences as vast as the world whence came the ancestors of Creole people. Owing largely to the African influence on Creole food, many dishes incorporate chilies—jambalaya and a crawfish boil come to mind—but Creole dishes tend not to be as spicy as those of their Cajun cousins. Nevertheless, hot sauce is a ubiquitous part of the New Orleans dining culture.

There is, of course, the fact of Tabasco's genesis in New Orleans, but that's not all. Many families in New Orleans keep a bottle of homemade hot sauce around the kitchen for regular use, often a bottle of vinegar steeped in chilies (same as the pepper sauce common in the Mississippi Delta). An untold number of kitschy gift shop hot sauces exist, with regional buzzwords worked into the labels, like "Mardi Gras," "Zydeco," and "Voodoo." CaJohn's even makes a commemorative (and uncharacteristically bad) Nola Hot Sauce.

One of the more unique hot sauces I've ever encountered and an instant favorite—it's just the thing to gussy up a po'boy—comes out of New Orleans and speaks to the city's Caribbean roots. Its maker, Tiffany Jensen, is a New Orleans native who in 1977 helped open Tipitina's, a revered Uptown juke joint on Tchoupitoulas Street in a building that was once a gambling house and brothel. (One gets the feeling just about every old building in New Orleans was at one time a gambling house and brothel.) Tipitina's was the home base for New Orleans piano legend Professor Longhair during his declining years (the venue's name comes from the title of a Professor Longhair song), and it has earned a reputation as a cornerstone of the New Orleans music scene. It has, perhaps unsurprisingly, never been known as a bastion of moderation. When Tiffany went on a three-week vacation to St. John, in the US Virgin Islands, she knew pretty quickly that when she came home, it wouldn't be for long.

"I thought I better go before I killed myself partying. I was having a very good time," she told me. She said her good-byes at Tipitina's and returned to St. John to stay indefinitely. She ended up making a life there. "I didn't mean to, but it was a nice twenty-five years."

From the start she felt oddly at home in the culture of St. John. "Their cooking is so interesting," she said. "They use a lot of the spices we use here in New Orleans, around this area. The Creole influence. A lot of thyme. Rice and beans. A lot of similarities."

In time she met her husband, Russell, and for medical reasons the two finally relocated back to New Orleans. The couple now makes a hot sauce reminiscent of St. John's island flavors, with homegrown habaneros and lemongrass—the most prominent flavor in Moko Jumbie hot sauce's unique profile—plus cayenne, cardamom, nutmeg, and about a dozen other spices.

The sauce is named for the *moko jumbie*, as they are known in much of the Caribbean, performers of an ancient West African tradition that show up during festivals, especially Carnival, throughout the region—in New Orleans people tend to call them stilt walkers.

"They're like the deities from Africa. They're supposed to keep the evil spirits away," Tiffany said. "I guess they just make me feel like a kid again. And it's got a great ring."

Moko Jumbie is available online, but it can only be bought at two brick-and-mortar locations: the Saturday morning farmer's market in Olde Town Slidell, just outside New Orleans, and Parasol's, a sixty-plus-year-old neighborhood watering hole and eatery in the Irish Channel.*

---

* *Warning:* I paid twice as much for a bottle of Moko Jumbie at Parasol's than Tiffany charges at the farmer's market in Slidell. Admittedly, the Parasol's chef may have just been punishing me after I clumsily got him busted for dosing a coworker's drink with hot sauce, as in, "Hey, are you pouring Tabasco in that iced tea!?" Despite my faux pas, you can often find me—and Moko Jumbie—at Parasol's.

With so much hot sauce on offer and the presence of the world-wide heavyweight champion—Tabasco—right nearby, a person could wonder if there is a New Orleans favorite. Wonder no more.

Terrance Tyrell is a New Orleans native with deep roots in the city—"I've never heard of my family being from anywhere else," he told me. On a Wednesday like any other, he sat down for a lunch of red beans with rice at Frankie and Johnny's, a staple Creole restaurant in Uptown New Orleans. Traditionally red beans were eaten on Monday, laundry day, because a woman could cook them without much tending to while also washing clothes, but folks have washing machines now and eat red beans any old day of the week. Terrance took a picture of his meal and posted it on Facebook with the following caption: "Question. Tabasco, Crystal or Louisiana . . . Which goes better with #RedBeans? LOL ;D"

The post warranted an LOL because he knew he was about to start what has come to be known in the popular vernacular as a "shit-storm." Opinions were opined. Exclamation points exclaimed. In the end, Louisiana had a strong showing and Tabasco wasn't without its devotees, but the clear winner was the one Tyrell said he doused over his beans even before putting up his cheeky Facebook post: Crystal, New Orleans's hot sauce hometown hero.

Per company history, in 1923 Alvin Baumer was in love with Mildred Bacher. Sadly for Alvin, before he could tie the knot he lost his job, rendering him less than marriage material in the eyes of Mildred's family. Undaunted, Alvin showed some of the biggest stones ever shown by a man in love and asked his future father-in-law for a loan to buy a small business that made syrup for sno-balls (a New Orleans thing—it's basically a softer, fluffier version of what most Americans call a snow cone). The loan went through, and among the papers that came with his new business was a recipe for Crystal Pure Louisiana Hot Sauce. The provenance of the recipe is apocryphal, but Crystal's total of three ingredients—cayenne peppers, vinegar, and salt—suggests it wasn't all that descriptive anyway. The resulting hot sauce is quite mild, roughly half as hot as Tabasco, or less, though Baumer Foods does make an extra-hot version.

Crystal hot sauce was first made on Tchoupitoulas Street before Baumer Foods relocated to a facility on Tulane Avenue, where the company's iconic sign became a New Orleans landmark. Terrance Tyrell worked there in his younger days on the factory line. In 2005 Hurricane Katrina destroyed the sign and the factory. After the storm, a replica of the sign was placed atop the old factory building, but Baumer Foods moved all production to Reserve, Louisiana, a community about thirty miles upriver, which, as the company is sure to note on its website, "is 9 feet above sea level."

Tabasco is a major force in New Orleans, to be sure, but most locals are loyal to the home team, Crystal. As for me, in this as in other aspects of life I am an apostate—I prefer to mix them.

10

THE LAST DASH

In some ways, suffering ceases to be suffering at the moment
it finds a meaning, such as the meaning of a sacrifice.
—Viktor Frankl, *Man's Search for Meaning*

Only one state in America has an official state question. Californians might ask each other "beach or mountains?"; and in Louisiana you're bound to overhear someone say "fried or boiled?"; and in Washington, DC, every other suit wakes up in the morning, walks to the tie rack, and asks himself "blue or red?" But only one state has made a query official. By an act of the legislature in 1996, New Mexico declared its official state question to be one that servers at New Mexican restaurants probably find themselves muttering in their sleep.

"Red or green?"

They're asking whether you want red chile* sauce or green chile sauce slathered over your food. And there's even a secret answer: if, like me, you prefer both red and green chile, just say "Christmas!"

---

* Out of deference to New Mexican culture, in this section I have adopted the spelling "chile," as is common in New Mexico, home to the Chile Pepper Institute. New Mexico can call fruits of the genus *Capsicum* whatever it wants.

and your enchiladas will come out drenched in yuletide colors, unless it's actually Christmastime, in which case if you're in New Mexico, you're probably eating tamales, not enchiladas, and it is they that will get the two-chile treatment.

I'd been traveling across New Mexico by car for several days with the original hot sauce Nicks himself, my father, heretofore referred to by the sobriquet I bestowed upon him years ago, Two Shack. The name is a tribute to the two dilapidated neighboring lakeside shacks of which he was once the proud owner (and which he still owns today, it's just that he long ago renovated them to cottage status). We were going slow and stopping often for New Mexican grub enlivened by or built entirely around the state's beloved Hatch chiles: Christmas enchiladas, green chile cheese-burgers, green chile pizzas, more Christmas enchiladas, and Two Shack's favorite, *chiles rellenos*. As food travel goes, we were getting a pretty immersive green chile experience, such that Two Shack's stomach started acting up under the unceasing barrage of capsaicin, but he pressed onward undaunted. Not much more than a beer was ingested without green chile, and even then we had the option; more than one New Mexico brewery makes a beer with the state's favorite plant, like the Taos Green Chile Beer from Eske's Brew Pub and Eatery.

But we were not in New Mexico merely to eat green chile and drink beer. I had invited Two Shack along on what was a kind of pilgrimage. We had a lunch date in Albuquerque with America's spicy food oracle, the Chaplain of Chiles, the High Septon of Hot Sauce, the Pope of Peppers—the legendary Dave DeWitt.

At his suggestion, we met DeWitt for lunch at El Pinto, a restau-rant on a thirteen-acre spread in north Albuquerque serving classic New Mexican fare that DeWitt said was the best in the state, making El Pinto, by extrapolation, purveyors of the some of the finest New

Mexican food there is. We parked and walked toward the entrance, past a decommissioned army jeep and a veritable Eden of luscious potted greenery. We were early and waited near the entrance for DeWitt to arrive, occupying ourselves with a survey of photographs on the walls of El Pinto's twin brother co-owners next to an impressive variety of celebrities: Katy Perry, Snoop Dogg, Playboy Bunny Amy Leigh Andrews, former congressman Ron Paul, Lil Wayne (twice), and one picture, bravely displayed, with members of Nickleback.

DeWitt was impossible to miss. Like Two Shack, he wore shorts and a short-sleeve Hawaiian-style shirt, only his was patterned entirely in red and green chilies. On his key ring hung a small cylinder that he calls his "burn pod," a receptacle containing habanero powder in case of bland food emergency. We took our seats at a table on one of El Pinto's many patios and consulted with DeWitt about what to order.

"Their chiles rellenos aren't very good, I'll tell you that," he said. Apparently the kitchen cooks them and holds them for a few minutes instead of sending them straight from the fryer to the table, as God intended, "which means they're not the best they could be. But everything else is great."

At DeWitt's urging Two Shack and I ordered, to share: a bowl of *posole*, a New Mexican (and regular Mexican) stew with pork, hominy, and red chile; *carne adovada*, pork marinated in red chile and spices and served in a tortilla, with sides of pinto beans and rice; and red chile ribs, an extremely simple recipe of baby back ribs marinated overnight in nothing but red chile and a tiny bit of sea salt, then slow baked, marinated again, and briefly seared, resulting in what DeWitt declares (he's quoted on the menu), "The best ribs in the world!" We washed it all down with beers and warm sopaipillas dripping in honey.

I can't speak for those chiles rellenos, but every bite we ordered was outstanding.

Dave DeWitt may be the go-to guy on New Mexican cuisine, but he started his career far from the American Southwest. He grew up in Virginia and worked in media, producing radio and television commercials in Richmond when, in July 1974, he took a vacation to New Mexico. On that visit some New Mexican friends served him a spicy green chile stew. "I started sweating and hiccupping, and the whole thing, but I hung in there, managed to finish the bowl to the applause of everybody," he told me. "They actually spiced it up more than normal.

"I completely fell in love with the state," he said.

By November that year he'd uprooted and moved to New Mexico. He began writing books about chiles, both solo and in collaboration with others, and in the 1980s organized the National Fiery Foods & Barbecue Show, which still claims the title of the largest spicy food show on earth.

"When we started it, there were no other shows," DeWitt said. "A couple of festivals like the Whole Enchilada Festival down in Las Cruces, but other than festivals, there was no real trade show involving chile peppers." In the mid-1990s DeWitt and Chuck Evans collaborated on *The Hot Sauce Bible* and the publisher's publicist started billing DeWitt as the Pope of Peppers. The name stuck.

"I thought maybe it would offend the Italians when I went over to Italy," DeWitt told me. "Nah. They loved it. The old Papa del Pepperocini, they call me."

I asked DeWitt for the defining characteristics of New Mexican cuisine.

"Basically it's a corn, beans, squash, chile cuisine," he said. "Four main ingredients in it, and they're done in many different ways. But New Mexico is famous for its chile peppers. Immature they're green and mature they're red, and they form the basis of the cuisine and are the primary difference between New Mexican cuisine and the cuisine of neighboring states. For example, you've heard of Tex-Mex?"

"Right."

"You've heard of Sonoran style. Well when they make their sauces, they thicken their sauces with things like flour or cornstarch. We don't do that in New Mexico. A chile sauce has onions, chiles, and water, and that's just about it."

Sitting there at the table with Dave and Two Shack, I felt a distinct sense of getting back to the basics, nearer the origin of things, and not just because I was with the fella from whose eye twinkle I was once spawned. Even if chile peppers were introduced to New Mexico by the Spanish—an idea of which I am not wholly convinced—the state's watery but flavorful, pure green chile sauce has a direct lineage to the early-evolutionary-stage hot sauces prepared by native people in the Americas before Columbus bumped into the continent, like the simple llajwa sauce eaten by Bolivians. In New Mexican green chile you can taste the vegetable matter, and even the water, like a spiced-up version of the simple red chile stew I had at the Tiwa Kitchen near the Taos Pueblo. Appropriately, we were eating at a restaurant with a relatively long history in Albuquerque that may go back to the beginning, in at least one sense, of New Mexican cuisine itself.

Today, El Pinto is the largest restaurant in New Mexico, though it doesn't feel that way. Each room and patio opens up to another room and patio, none oppressively large and with greenery all around, such that every table feels steps away from an unseen garden. This effect is a natural outgrowth of the fact that it was built piece by piece.

El Pinto began in the early 1960s when Albuquerque's population was a third of what it is today, as ten tables in a room connected to a country house, with five kids living in one bedroom and two parents in the other, in an empty valley north of town. On a summer evening in 1961 a Hungarian American former World War II POW drinking a scotch and soda on his patio asked his Spanish-speaking New Mexican wife, "Honey, how would you say 'the spot,' like 'This is the spot,' in Spanish?"

"El Pinto," she said—like a pinto horse.

That became the name of the restaurant they opened out of their home a year later. After high school their two youngest sons, the twins John and Jim Thomas, moved to Alaska to work in construction, and when they came home a few years later, they went to work in their parents' restaurant, eventually buying mom and dad out. Over the years they used their building know-how to add on a room here, a patio there, and slowly bought up surrounding tracts of land. They prepared food based on recipes handed down from their grandmother, Josephine Chevas Griggs, who, they say, coined the term *New Mexican food* back in 1939, a claim that I cannot confirm nor disprove but that I can wholeheartedly admire for its audacity. Today Jim and John run a big and growing restaurant that cooks for hundreds like it's cooking for a handful, only dozens of times every hour.

El Pinto sources its chiles from farms in the southern part of the state around Hatch, the town that gives its name to the chiles for which New Mexico is famous. Around El Pinto's expansive estate Jim and John have small experiments in vegetable growing underway, but their most intensive agricultural operation is a worm farm. Discarded vegetable matter from the kitchen is put in plastic barrels with a little starter soil and worms, which work their digestive magic on the lettuce cuttings and avocado husks and so forth until they render a kind of microorganism-rich compost juice that Jim Thomas calls "nutrient-rich tea."

Two Shack and I were led on a quick tour of the worm farm along with a group of Walgreens employees—still unclear on why they were there—during which our tour guide opened one of the barrels to show off El Pinto's worm herd. Our guide put on rubber gloves as he explained the worms' digestive process and how occasionally someone comes in to stir the soil. I've come to know Two Shack pretty well over the past several decades, and I had visions of him sinking his bare hands into the muck to churn a handful of worms and putrefying garbage. Moments later, Two Shack walked up to the barrel and sunk his bare hands into the muck to churn a handful of worms and putrefying garbage, lifting out a rich and squirming handful. The Walgreens employees and tour guide were a little aghast. I wasn't. The worm farm is an impressive operation.

The worm tea is regularly drained from the barrels and transported to the farms they work with down south, where farmers spray it on the chile crop in lieu of chemical pesticides and fertilizers.

"A lot of people go farm to table," Jim said as we finished lunch, chewing sopaipillas with honey. "Everybody understands that term. What we do is actually kind of the opposite—we actually go table to farm."

Hatch, New Mexico, is famous for one thing—the chiles that bear its name—but that may soon change. When driving into town, you pass roadside stands selling *ristras*, long hanging strands of dried or drying chiles, and surrounding fields with rows and rows of chile plants, but the most striking feature of the place is the giants.

Today Hatch is home to what is undoubtedly one of the biggest concentrations of large-scale kitsch in America: enormous fiberglass cartoon sculptures in the style of midcentury Americana fast-food mascots, like the iconic Kip's Big Boy statues. Over the past several years the married couple that owns the quirky restaurant Sparky's has been buying and installing the statues all over town. The effect is totally bizarre, like being in a tiny farming town within a kooky sculpture garden, which come to think of it is exactly what Hatch is. There's a statue of Yogi Bear. There's the massive bucket of KFC chicken with two dancing chiles on top. There are waiters hoisting burgers and root beers on the roof of Sparky's. There's even a thirty-foot statue of Uncle Sam cradling a green chile. And many more.

As tourist attractions the statues could become as important as the chiles in years to come. The number of acres of chiles under cultivation in New Mexico has fallen year on year since 1992. The decline is part of a wider trend throughout the United States—according to the US Department of Agriculture, 19,100 acres of chiles were harvested in the United States in 2014, a 40 percent decline since 2000. The main culprit is the cost of farm labor, specifically the cost of paying people to pick chiles during the harvest. Farmers in New Mexico have been particularly affected since the implementation in 1994 of the North American Free Trade Agreement by competition from Mexican farms, which can pay far lower wages to pickers than American farms can afford, but globalization isn't the only cause of the decline. The McIlhenny family outsources its tabasco pepper cultivation to farms in Latin America and Africa because it long ago couldn't afford to pay pickers to harvest chiles on and around Avery Island. Until 1938, Louisiana led the country in chile pepper production, but after the Second World War the oil and gas industry came to the state in force, providing jobs with far higher wages than a chile farm could match. By 1978, chile production in the state had dropped by 75 percent, and by 1998 commercial chile pepper farming in Louisiana had practically vanished.

The challenge for chile farmers is that it's extremely difficult to build a machine capable of efficiently harvesting chiles. Pepper picking takes dexterity and nuance, a human touch. Different pods ripen at different times on a plant, so the harvest requires multiple passes of the same rows without damaging the plants or harvesting unripe pods. Further complicating the matter, the strength with which a pod at any given stage of ripening is attached to the stem varies from plant to plant. Pickers get a feel for picking chiles over time, knowing how hard to pull without tearing apart a plant and how to remove ripe chiles without pulling off unripe pods. In the case of small chiles, like tabasco peppers, the pods are very small and delicate, so pickers don't always wear gloves, leaving their hands exposed to the burn of capsaicin. It's hard, low-paying work. Attempts to mechanize chile harvesting in a way that is efficient and preserves the quality of the fruit have been largely unsuccessful, with the exception of machines built for some varieties, like jalapeños and bell peppers. But scientists and engineers make progress on the question every day, and a break-through harvester could come to the rescue of New Mexico's chile farmers while simultaneously undercutting what little livelihood the pickers make as it is.

In *Desert Solitaire*, Edward Abbey writes, "The extreme clarity of the desert light is equaled by the extreme individuation of desert life forms. Love flowers best in openness and freedom." After traveling the country thinking about hot sauce—this peculiar table condiment that brings out the sadomasochist in so many of us—it seemed time to head to the desert. Hot sauce represents a kind of desert flower, after all, most loved and most entrenched among the most downtrodden people on earth. Time and again we find it's the people most familiar with the rawest pain who most cherish the pain-inducing condiment: enslaved African Americans, Cajuns, Mexican migrant laborers. Mississippi has the highest poverty rate in the United States. New Mexico has the second highest. Louisiana has the third highest. Can it be a coincidence that America's hot sauce hot spots are also some of its most impoverished places? Europeans introduced the chile to Africa and Asia, but it was the colonized and not the colonizers who most passionately incorporated chiles into their cuisines. Why does hot sauce flourish amid suffering?

Two Shack and I headed southwest out of Hatch toward El Paso, where we filled up the car's gas tank. The next stretch promised to be desolate.

A light sprinkle fell as we exited the gas station. We pointed the car toward Marfa, and a rainbow presented itself from the horizon before us over the vast wasteland of West Texas. Minutes later the rain picked up, slowly then quickly into an awful downpour. The sky darkened, night fell, and traffic on the interstate slowed to a crawl, like a wagon train of eighteen-wheelers and smaller vehicles interspersed here and there. There was lightning in the distance in all directions, the mountains flat and black against the high desert horizon like painted set pieces in a dark high school play. We passed an eighteen-wheeler, which had been headed in the opposite direction, turned over on its left side. Then another. And another. In the end we solemnly rolled by five eighteen-wheelers all turned over identically on their left sides, like some vindictive tornado god with the heart of a toddler came rampaging up the interstate from the direction in which we were then headed. Finally, we turned off I-10 onto Route 90 and drove with the storm into the darkness toward Marfa.

Marfa, Texas, began in the late nineteenth century as a railroad water stop, and truth be told the layout of town hasn't developed too far beyond that. With a population of roughly two thousand today, Marfa is situated where Route 67 crosses Route 90 in the Big Bend region, the section of the Chihuahuan high desert where the Rio Grande dips toward Mexico then back north into the United States to form the iconic shovel shape of West Texas. Driving toward Marfa, I kept thinking of the Rub' al-Khali, the enormous zone of barren sand in the southern part of the Arabian Peninsula also known ominously as the Empty Quarter. The comparison is an overstatement—we're talking arid, scrubby soil, not sand dunes—but the point is that the place evokes an overwhelming sense of bleak, immense isolation. Marfa is the sort of town small enough to have totally clear boundaries, such that one step beyond the far side of Waco Street or Missouri Street or Aprejo Street, and you are definitively outside the society of humankind and if not in the actual wilderness then at least on the wild side of a stark divide.

What lies within those boundaries is a peculiar blend of art-world cool and tumbleweed quiet that has made Marfa famous over the many decades since a New York City artist moved to this nowhere town to turn the desert into a permanent art gallery.

Marfa was the site of an army airfield during the Second World War that was decommissioned shortly after the war ended. During his stint in the army after the war, a Missouri-born man named Donald Judd passed through Marfa, and the memory of the place stuck with him as he launched a career as an artist in the 1950s and '60s. In the 1970s, disillusioned with the New York art world and with the ephemeral essence of temporary art exhibitions, Judd was on the lookout for a place that could host permanent installations. He remembered Marfa.

In time, Judd bought the barracks and other abandoned buildings of the army base just outside of town, turning the surrounding landscape into a canvas for his megalith-sized minimalist sculptures. I spent an enjoyable afternoon walking around and among Judd's series of fifteen angular works in concrete, groups of identical, enormous rectangular blocks assembled in different abstract arrangements. Two Shack puzzled doggedly over how, exactly, Judd managed the logistics of the project (Two Shack is something of a concrete connoisseur) and what, in the hell, it was for.

Donald Judd died in 1994, but the movement he started is now moving under its own power. Marfa today is brimming with art and artists. A pop-up faux Prada store beside the highway outside of town is probably Marfa's most famous installation, but the art is everywhere, such that at least one public trash can is painted with the words THIS IS NOT ART to make sure visitors don't get confused and decline to use it. These days the town is an odd juxtaposition of its middle of nowhereness and a sense of connection to faraway cultural centers like Los Angeles, New York City, Miami during Art Basel, and so forth. At times Marfa can feel like a long-lost neighborhood somewhere deep in a forgotten Brooklyn desert.

As with all good things, people who have been to Marfa before you love to talk about how Marfa is over, passé now, ruined by hipsters. Don't believe them. Whenever people tell you about how much cooler something once was than it is now, they are by definition talking about a time when they were younger and probably thinner. People say this about everything, and it's always bullshit. It's your cue to steal their nose, laugh at their defeatism, and go dancing off into the sunset toward whatever adventure you had in mind in the first place.

Two Shack and I went for lunch at the Thunderbird Hotel, where I'd heard there was a hot sauce with an exceedingly strange name available at the attached restaurant. After first introducing me to her pet praying mantis, the young woman behind the front desk confirmed that yes, I was in the right place, the restaurant was open, and the chef was there serving up his signature Two Dick Billy Goat Hot Sauce.

For lunch, I ordered the steak topped with a poached egg and scallions with a side of thick-cut fried potatoes. Two Shack had the fried chicken with mashed potatoes and a biscuit. Both dishes were mouth-drenchingly delicious and shockingly high brow, plated more like something you'd get at a West Village bistro than a hotel at a high desert highway crossing, two hundred miles from the nearest airport of any consequence (El Paso). Both dishes came out with a ramekin filled with a thick and luscious orange hot sauce.

"I'd put that up there with some of the best fried chicken I've ever had," Two Shack said as he poured his leftover hot sauce out onto his plate and began sifting through it with a knife and fork.

"Breakin' down de hot sauce," he said quietly and to no one. "It's mighteleh gooood." He was focused intently on the science project then under way on his plate. After a minute he looked up.

"Does he market this sauce, or . . .?"

"I don't know," I said. "That'll be one of my first questions."

Mark Scott was born in New Orleans. When he was eleven, the family moved to his mom's hometown, Marfa, after his grandfather fell ill and the crime rate reached distressing levels in Orleans Parish.

"That was just the hugest culture shock ever," he told me. "There's no trees, there's no water, there's no diversity in the school system. It's like, 'Where did everyone go, and where are the trees?'"

What Marfa lacked in big-city amenities it made up for in small-town charm. Whereas in New Orleans Mark wasn't allowed to leave the driveway, in Marfa he and friends ran free all over town until his mother rang a bell in the front yard around dusk. After graduating high school he moved around a bit—a stint in Austin, a stint in Florida—but he always came back to Marfa, and eventually he came back to stay. "This place sucks a lot of the time," he told me. "But it doesn't suck nearly as much as most other places. If you can get used to not having the everyday comforts of life, then Marfa is definitely a great place to live."

Mark worked in kitchens around Marfa for several years before he and his wife opened their own food truck, Fat Lyle's. Sometime circa 2010, a friend of his brought a hot sauce back from the Caribbean,

Pirate's Revenge (from Eleuthera island in the Bahamas). It was unlike any of the thicker, more vinegary sauces of the Southwest or southern Louisiana he'd grown up with. "This was a whole different world. It's not southern, it's not like the hot sauces around here," he said. "And then it was gone. And there was no more." He determined to try to re-create the sweet-hot sauce his friend had discovered, and those experiments are what eventually became the goopy blend of habaneros, peaches, molasses, and brown sugar that he calls Two Dick Billy Goat Hot Sauce. The name, he says, comes from a saying of indeterminate hillbilly provenance: "hotter than a two dick billy goat fucking in a forest fire." For a brief time he also made a green hot sauce called Two Rats (hotter than two rats fucking in a tube sock, in case you're curious), though it has been discontinued. Two Dick Billy Goat is generally available only at the Thunderbird Hotel and from time to time at the Marfa farm stand, where Mark sells it to turn an extra buck when he feels so moved. Two Shack was utterly taken with the sauce, and Mark was kind enough to put some in a jar for my old man to take home.

On the way out of town Two Shack and I stopped for beers at the Lost Horse Saloon off Route 90, a few-frills beer joint (in some places they'd call it a honky-tonk) with an impressively destroyed piano and a refreshingly unpolished vibe. We drank beers in the patio out back while storm clouds gathered on the horizon. A cowboy with an eye patch—I'm not kidding—sat silently in the corner drinking a beer with a dog at his feet. It was quiet.

"I think in terms of finding a cool ending for your book," my dad said. "Well, it's like, the best hot sauce in the nation is in Marfa, Texas. But you can't get any. You gotta go there to get some."

So, there you have it. Two Shack has made it official: his favorite hot sauce is Two Dick Billy Goat made by Mark Scott in Marfa, Texas.

We had one more stop on our journey, and so we traveled on, heading eastbound out of town. We spent the night in Alpine, the gateway to Big Bend National Park. In the morning we turned south down State Highway 118 deeper into the desert wilderness and toward a remote town on the far reaches of the perimeter described to us by locals as a place "at the end of the world," a ghost town called Terlingua, about fifteen miles north of the Rio Grande and the Mexican border.

The irony of Terlingua is that it's called a ghost town but people do live there. They're just camped in dwellings in various states of completion between or within the ruins of old long-abandoned mud brick houses. The town even has a major tourist event, the Original Terlingua International Championship Chili Cookoff.

But down the road just fifteen minutes is a "town," if you can call it that, right on the Rio Grande and the Mexican border, where what locals there are elected as their mayor a beer-drinking billy goat named Clay Henry. Aside from a bar, a general store, a few odd buildings, and a totally out-of-place golf resort with an acid-trippily weird Disneyfied Old West Main Street utterly devoid of human life, there doesn't seem to be anyone, or very many people, at least, who actually live there. In the horror movie version of these two towns, the teenagers avoid the Terlingua ghost town and seek refuge in Lajitas, only to find that the weirdly polished town where they've sought refuge is the haunted one.

Terlingua is an actual community. The general store has a generic hot sauce labeled Terlingua Hot Sauce for its gift shop, where they also sell Fairhope Favorite's Moonshine Hot Sauce (in its form packaged as dynamite, or "redneck fishing lure"). There's a woman in town who makes a local dipping salsa called India's Hot Salsa, which she prepares in the kitchen of the Starlight Theatre, next door to the general store. I couldn't track down the maker, but I did learn that the massive nude painting at the Thirsty Goat Saloon in Lajitas is of her, decades ago.

Still, even if it's not quite a ghost town, Terlingua is supremely isolated. It's a two-hour drive from Alpine, the nearest real town, through some of the most rugged, desolate terrain America has to offer. And Alpine is itself two and a half hours from Midland-Odessa, the nearest municipality with a serious airport.

Two Shack and I bought a couple of beers in Terlingua and took a seat in the shade in front of the general store. A cowboy sat on a bench at the far end of the long porch. He would have looked cartoonish, with his pants tucked into his boots and a feather in his wide, round, flat-brimmed hat, had he not been tinkering knowingly with a leather horse bridle. He'd worked as a pilot somewhere for thirty years before retiring to the Big Bend area, he said. It was quiet, and the sun shone fiercely over the desert and ocher ruins, skeletons of buildings with long-forgotten purposes scattered in all directions. The cowboy put aside the bridle, pulled out a set of bagpipes, and began to play.

Two Shack's phone started making noises, jarring all of us on the porch. He chuckled at a video playing on the screen.

"That almost sounds like Aric Queen's voice," he said, laughing to himself as he pressed the volume-down button. After a minute he got up and walked off to wander among the ruins.

The cowboy stopped playing and huffed quietly to himself. He was irritated.

One does not arrive at a place like Terlingua, so cut off from the hum, bustle, tears, and laughs of human society, because one had an especially easy go of it wherever one came from. You get the feeling that the sort of person who takes up residence in a place as hardscrabble as an old ghost town deep in the West Texas desert has seen pain in his past. But that, of course, is true of all of us. Our pain speaks to us in the crucible of our own consciousness, in memories of the trials that make us who we are, echoing in our daily lives, our choices, our preferences.

As a young man, Friedrich Nietzsche discovered the work of the philosopher Arthur Schopenhauer, a dour pessimist who believed that life is suffering and that the best a human can hope for is to live ascetically, minimizing pain by striving for pleasure as little as possible. Nietzsche held to this worldview for many years, until an invitation to spend the winter with a group of fellow writers at an Italian villa near Sorrento sparked a radical transformation.

Nietzsche was in poor health when he traveled to Italy, but he came alive during those months in the Mediterranean sun, living among friends in a villa with views of the Gulf of Naples and Mount Vesuvius in the distance. He discovered within himself a new lust for life that contravened Schopenhauer's admonition to lay low and renounce pleasure.

Nietzche's outlook on life underwent a total metamorphosis. He kept Schopenhauer's focus on the importance of pain in our lives, but he came to view pain differently, not as an intrinsic evil to be avoided but as an inseparable constituent of joy. This included the agony of both psychological pain and physical pain. He began to regularly deploy the metaphor of mountain climbing, an activity rewarding in direct proportion to the pain and difficulty of the climb. Nietzsche came to view pain as not an unfortunate and unavoidable part of life but as inseparable from pleasure, and in particular from the pleasure that comes from achieving greatness.

Not long after his stay in southern Italy, Nietzsche published *The Gay Science*, a work produced, he writes stirringly, in "the jubilation of returning strength, of a reawakened faith in a tomorrow and a day after tomorrow, of a sudden sense and anticipation of a future, of impending adventures, of reopened seas, of goals that are permitted and believed in again."

In *The Gay Science*, Nietzsche articulates his new position on pain. "But what if pleasure and pain should be so closely connected that he who wants the greatest possible amount of the one must also have the greatest possible amount of the other, that he who wants to experience the 'heavenly high jubilation,' must also be ready to be 'sorrowful unto death'?"

Nietzsche admonishes us to abandon lives of safety and comfort—and, if I may, of boring, unchallenging food—because "the secret for harvesting from existence the greatest fruitfulness and the greatest enjoyment is—*to live dangerously*! Build your cities on the slopes of Vesuvius! Send your ships into uncharted seas! Live at war with your peers and yourselves! Be robbers and conquerors as long as you cannot be rulers and possessors, you seekers of knowledge!"

Who, after reading that, cannot appreciate the value of pain? Who can resist the urge now *to live dangerously*?

The simple truth is that pain embeds itself deeper in our inner-most minds than joy. This is why you can't quite get back to the blinding excitement you felt when you got your first bicycle, but dwelling on any given high school humiliation is likely to make your chest tighten and a lump settle in your throat.

Only a liar or a psychopath would tell you this relationship to pain isn't a burden, but for humans, equipped with our ability to analyze abstractions, it's also a tremendous gift. Pain hammers and scrapes us into finer forms, marking our bodies and personalities like the scarred contours of an ancient canyon. Since suffering is inextrica-bly linked to pleasure, pain records on our behalf the most cherished events of our lives. Should you one day summit Everest, you will remember the struggle of the climb. If you master the violin it will be because painful, tedious practice has implanted those skills in your fingers. When a romance ends, the love that once held you warmly entangled with a partner may one day grow faint, but you will never lose access to the pain of what was lost. In the throbbing memory you can still conjure the circumference of her hips, the weight of his hand, the remnants of sleep in her eyes.

It may be that the human is the only animal that eats hot sauce for pleasure—and that cultures most recently acquainted with suffering are those that hold hot sauce most dear—because of our unique relationship to pain. Unsatisfied with experiencing pain and letting it go, we live burdened and blessed by the drive to make sense of it. We need pain to mean something, so we play with it in small, safe ways. We watch horror movies. We relish the sting of the tattoo gun. And we drench our food in hot sauce—to enliven our meals and to dance with pain, the indispensable creative force in our lives, affirming our humanity and staking a claim to our ineffable place in the cosmos.

After a while, the cowboy resumed playing, this time a wistful cowboy ballad on a guitar. I picked up another guitar leaning against the wall and began picking a soft melody along with him. He smiled a little and sang.

"Yodle-eheeee, yodle-eheeee, yodle-eheeeeeeee."

SELECTED
BIBLIOGRAPHY

Alley, Thomas R., and Jeffrey W. Burroughs. "Do Men Have Stronger Preferences for Hot, Unusual, and Unfamiliar Foods?" *Journal of General Psychology* 118, no. 3(1991), 201–215.

Andrews, Jean. *Peppers: The Domesticated Capsicums.* Austin: University of Texas Press, 1995.

Bian, Zheng, Junshi Chen, Yiping Chen, Zhemngming Chen, Jianwei Du, Pengfei Ge, Yu Guo, Wei Hou, Yanjie Li, Liming Li, et al. "Consumption of Spicy Foods and Total and Cause Specific Mortality: Population Based Cohort Study." *BMJ* 351, no. h3942 (2015).

Brown, Cecil H., et al. "The Paleobiolinguistics of Domesticated Chili Pepper (*Capsicum* spp.)." *Ethnobiology Letters* 4 (August 2013): 1–11.

Byrnes, Nadia K., and John E. Hayes. "Personality Factors Predict Spicy Food Liking and Intake." *Food Quality and Preference* 28, no. 1 (April 1, 2013): 213–221. www.ncbi.nlm.nih.gov/pmc/articles/PMC3607321/?report=reader.

Caterina, M. J., M. A. Schumacher, M. Tominaga, T. A. Rosen, J. D. Levine, and D. Julius. "The Capsaicin-Receptor: A Heat-Activated Ion Channel in the Pain Pathway." *Nature* 389 (October 23, 1997): 816–824.

Cavanaugh, Jack. "Savannah Dining: Angel's Serves Up Heavenly Barbecue." *Savannah Morning News*, March 22, 2014.

Center for Drug Evaluation and Research. App Number 50-818, "Tobradex ST." February 6, 2009.

Columbus, Christopher. "Journal of the First Voyage of Columbus." Document AJ-062. Wisconsin Historical Society, 1942.

Comisión Nacional Pare El Desarrollo de los Puebelos Indígenas. "Indicadores sociodemográficos de la población indigena 2000–2005." September 2006. www.cdi.gob.mx/cedulas/sintesis _resultados_2005.pdf.

Diaz, Eddie. "The History of the Green Chile." Diaz Farms website. http://diazfarms.com/about.

Esmonde, Donn. "'Lost' Wing Pioneer Is Found." *Buffalo News*, July 13, 2013.

Ferdman, Roberto A., and Ritchie King. "The American Hot Sauce Craze in One Mouth Watering Chart." Quartz. January 28, 2014. http://qz.com/171500/the-american-hot-sauce-craze-in-one-mouth-watering-chart/.

Fox, Jonathon. "Mexico's Indigenous Population." *Cultural Survival* 23, no. 1 (Spring 1999). www.culturalsurvival.org/ourpublications /csq/article/mexicos-indigenous-population.

Hu, Winnie. "Hot Peppers Becoming Cash Crop for Bronx Community Garden." NYTimes.com. June 19, 2015. www.nytimes .com/2015/06/20/nyregion/hot-peppers-becoming-a-cash-crop -for-bronx-community-gardens.html?_r=0.

Kraft, Kraig H., Cecil H. Brown, Gary P. Nabhan, Eike Luedeling, José de Jesús Luna Ruiz, Geo Coppens d'Eeckenbrugge, Robert J. Hijmans, and Paul Gepts. "Multiple Lines of Evidence for the Origin of Domesticated Chili Pepper, *Capsicum annuum*, in Mexico." *PNAS* 111, no. 17 (2014): 6,165–6,170.

Lim, T. K. *Edible Medicinal and Non-Medicinal Plants*. Vol. 6, *Fruits*. New York: Springer Science & Business Media, 2013.

Massey, Douglas S., and Karen A. Pren. "Unintended Consequences of US Immigration Policy: Explaining the Post-1965 Surge from Latin America." *Population and Development Review* 38, no. 1 (2012): 1–29.

Meathead. "How to Make DC Mumbo Sauce (Or Is It Really Chicago Mumbo Sauce?)." Huffpost Taste. March 26, 2012. www.huffingtonpost.com/craig-goldwyn/mumbo-sauce_b_1376194.html.

Miller, Wilbur R. *The Social History of Crime and Punishment in America*. Los Angeles: Sage, 2012.

Monllos, Kristiana. "Carl's Jr. Is Launching 'Fast-Food's Hottest Burger,' Designed by an Ad Agency." Adweek. March 25, 2015. www.adweek.com/news/advertising-branding/carls-jr-and-hardees-releases-fast-foods-hottest-burger-today-163674.

Mullin, Rick. "Red Hot Chilli Peppers: The Chemical Capsaicin Makes Peppers Hot; the Best Antidote May Be Ice Cream." *Chemical and Engineering News* 81, no. 44 (November 3, 2003): 41.

National Restaurant Association 2014 Culinary Forecast. www.restaurant.org/Downloads/PDFs/News-Research/WhatsHot/What-s-Hot-2014.pdf.

Oaklander, Mandy. "This One Condiment Instantly Improves Your Diet." *Time*. December 3, 2015. http://time.com/4133939/hot-sauce-chili-peppers/.

Pappas, Stephanie. "The New Yoga? Sadomasochism Leads to Altered States, Study Finds." Live Science. February 19, 2014. www.livescience.com/43502-sadomasochism-mind-alteration.html.

Perrottet, Tony. "What Makes Houston the Next Great American City?" Smithsonian.com. July 2013. www.smithsonianmag

.com/travel/what-makes-houston-the-next-great-american-city
-4870584/?no-ist.

Perry, Charles. "Where Did Hot Sauce Come From?" Lecture at
the Los Angeles Public Library. October 11, 2014.

Potts, Rolf. "Robert Johnson Sold His Soul to the Devil in Rosedale." *Rolf Potts' Vagabonding* (blog). June 26, 2015. www
.vagablogging.net/robert-johnson-sold-his-soul-to-the-devil-in
-rosedale-mississippi.html.

Schweid, Richard. *Hot Peppers: The Story of Cajuns and Capsicum.*
Chapel Hill: University of North Carolina Press, 1999.

Stockton-MacNeish, Richard. *Second Annual Report of the Tehuacan
Archaeological-Botanical Project.* A project supported by grants
in aid from: the National Science Foundation and the Rock-
efeller Foundation, published by the foundation, 1962. https://
ia801009.us.archive.org/19/items/secondannualrepo00rich
/secondannualrepo00rich.pdf.

Terasaki, Masaharu, and Sumio Imada. "Sensation Seeking and
Food Preferences." *Personality and Individual Differences* 9,
no. 1(December 1988): 97–93.

Tewksbury, Joshua J., Karen M. Reagan, Noelle J. Machnicki,
Tomás A. Carlo, David C. Haak, Alejandra Loren, Calderón
Peñaloza, and Douglas J. Levey. "Evolutionary Ecology of Pungency in Wild Chilies." *PNAS* 105, no. 33 (2008): 11,808–
11,811.

"Tournefort, Joseph Pitton de." *Complete Dictionary of Scientific
Biography.* 2008. Encyclopedia.com. www.encyclopedia.com
/doc/1G2-2830904348.html.

Trillin, Calvin. "An Attempt to Compile a Short History of the
Buffalo Chicken Wing." *The New Yorker.* August 25, 1980.
www.newyorker.com/magazine/1980/08/25/an-attempt-to
-compile-a-short-history-of-the-buffalo-chicken-wing.

Trimpop, R. M. *The Psychology of Risk Taking Behavior.* New York: Elsevier, 1994.

Turner, Jack. *Spice: The History of a Temptation.* New York: Knopf, 2008.

Umami Information Center. "Umami-Rich Food." www.umami info.com/2011/03/umami-rich-food-meat.php/#beef.

University of Cincinnati Academic Health Center. "Heat in Chili Peppers Can Ease Sinus Problems, Research Shows." ScienceDaily. August 26, 2011. www.sciencedaily.com/releases/2011/08 /110825164933.htm.

U.S. Bureau of the Census. "Population of 100 Largest Urban Places: 1850." www.census.gov/population/www/documentation /twps0027/tab08.txt.www.sciencedaily.com/releases/2011/08 /110825164933.htm.

USDA Vegetables 2000 Summary. January 2001.

USDA Vegetables 2014 Summary. January 2015.

Webber, Brad. "Argia B. Collins, 76: Restaurateur Created Mumbo Barbecue Sauce." ChicagoTribune.com. February 6, 2003. http:// articles.chicagotribune.com/2003-02-06/news/0302060247_1 _barbecue-sauce-mr-collins-tangy.

INDEX